VICKI BUTLER-HENDERSON'S 100 SEXIEST CARS

I dedicate this book to my parents, Guy and Valerie.

THIS IS A CARLTON BOOK

Published in 2010 by Carlton Books Limited
20 Mortimer Street
London W1T 3JW

A catalogue record for this title is available from the British Library.

ISBN 978 1 84732 638 6

PUBLISHER'S NOTE:
Prices listed are manufacturers' recommended prices at time of a car's first release.

Editorial Manager: Roland Hall
Design: Katie Baxendale, Sailesh Patel, Elle Ward
Jacket Design: Darren Jordan
Picture Research: Paul Langan
Production: Claire Hayward
Editorial Assistant: Alice Payne
Pit crew: Callum Adamson, Steve Behan, Lester Brown

Printed in Dubai

10 9 8 7 6 5 4 3 2 1

VICKI BUTLER-HENDERSON'S
100 SEXIEST CARS

THE HOTTEST 100!

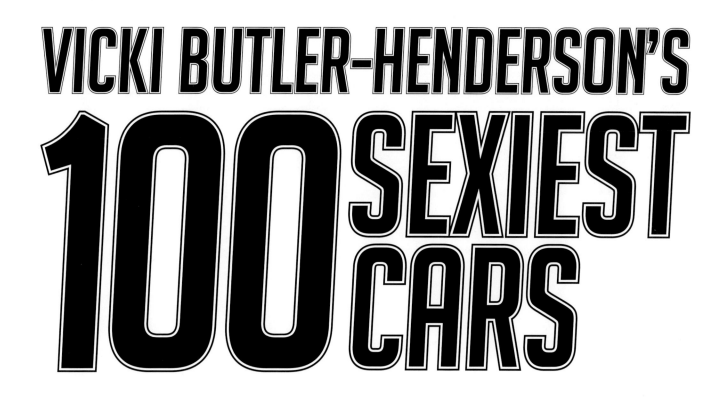

VICKI BUTLER-HENDERSON

CARLTON BOOKS

CONTENTS

INTRODUCTION 8

THE 100 SEXIEST CARS:

100 JAGUAR XK8 12

99 JAGUAR XKR 12

98 HUMMER...............................14

97 HONDA FCX CLARITY...............16

96 FORD MUSTANG 18

95 CHRYSLER VIPER....................20

94 DODGE CHARGER 22

93 FORD GRAN TORINO...............22

92 ASTON MARTIN DB7 24

91 AUDI TT 26

90 TESLA 30

89 ROLLS-ROYCE PHANTOM 32

88 MASERATI QUATTROPORTE.....34

87 FIAT 500 36

86 TROFEO ABARTH
     500 GB RACER 36

85 FORD CAPRI 38

84 LAND ROVER DEFENDER 40

83 LAND ROVER RANGE ROVER 40

82 ALFA ROMEO SZ 42

81 ALFA ROMEO RZ 42

80 FERRARI 308 GTS 46

79 FORD RACING PUMA 48

78 FORD PUMA 48

77 BMW Z8 50

76 BMW Z1 50

75 RENAULT ALPINE A610 TURBO 52

74 MERCEDES-BENZ SLS AMG 54

73 HOLDEN HSV 56

72 JAGUAR XJ220 58

71 MASERATI GRAN CABRIO 60

70 RENAULT CLIO 64

69 MEGANE RENAULTSPORT 250...64

68 VOLKSWAGEN GOLF GTI 66

67 PEUGEOT 205 GTI 66

66 BMW X5....................................68

65 BMW Z3 M COUPÉ 70

64 BMW Z4 70

63 NISSAN SKYLINE GT-R 72

62 TVR 74

61 NOBLE M400 76

60 RADICAL SR3 80

59 ARIEL ATOM 80

58 MERCEDES-BENZ SL65 AMG
   BLACK SERIES......................82

57 MAZDA MX-5 84

56 FORD GT 40 86

55 FORD GT 86

54 FERRARI 456....................88

53 BMW M1 90

52 LEXUS LF-A 92

51 MERCEDES-BENZ C63 AMG 94

50 PORSCHE CAYMAN 98

49 PORSCHE CAYENNE....................98

48 LOTUS EVORA.......................100

47 ALFA ROMEO 8C 102

46 ALFA ROMEO 8C SPIDER 102

45 BENTLEY CONTINENTAL
   GT SPEED 104

44 HONDA S2000 106

43 FERRAWWWRNIA 108

42 BUGATTI EB 110 110

41 CATERHAM SEVEN...................112

40 BMW F1 CAR 116

39 BMW M5..............................116

CONTENTS

38 ASTON MARTIN ONE-77 118

37 ASTON MARTIN VANQUISH S 120

36 MASERATI TROFEO 122

35 ASTON MARTIN DBS 124

34 ASTON MARTIN V8 VANTAGE 124

33 PORSCHE PANAMERA TURBO 126

32 PORSCHE BOXSTER 128

31 PAGANI ZONDA 130

30 NISSAN 350Z 134

29 NISSAN 370Z 134

28 MITSUBISHI EVO 136

27 MCLAREN MP4-12C 138

26 MERCEDES-BENZ

     SLR MCLAREN 138

25 HONDA NSX 140

24 FORD ESCORT COSWORTH ... 142

23 BMW M3 144

22 BMW M3 CABRIO 144

21 BMW M3 CSL.......................144

20 LANCIA DELTA

     INTEGRALE HF TURBO 148

19 MCLAREN F1 150

18 LAMBORGHINI GALLARDO 152

17 FERRARI 458 ITALIA 154

16 FERRARI F40 156

15 FERRARI ENZO 156

14 FERRARI F50 156

13 BENTLEY CONTINENTAL

     FLYING SPUR 158

12 AUDI R8...............................160

11 AUDI QUATTRO 162

10 A1 GP RACE CAR 166

9   PORSCHE CARRERA GT 168

8   LOTUS ELISE 170

7   LOTUS EXIGE....................170

6   LAMBORGHINI MURCIELAGO.. 172

5   FERRARI 430 174

4   FORMULA ONE 176

3   BUGATTI VEYRON..................178

2   PORSCHE 911 CARRERA S 180

1   LAMBORGHINI DIABLO GT 182

MORGAN 194

ROVER MGF 196

TWIN-ENGINED VW GOLF.............. 198

TRUCK RACER 200

GIBBS AQUADA BOAT CAR..........202

CITROEN 2CV 24-HOUR RACER....204

INDEX... 206

ACKNOWLEDGEMENTS................. 208

SO HOT THEY GET THEIR OWN LIST!

LAMBORGHINI GALLARDO LP570-4
SUPERLEGGERA 186

FERRARI 599 HGTE....................... 188

THE BAD AND THE... WEIRD

INTRODUCTION

Before I was born I think I was destined to drive cars. I like to think that I actually came into this world sideways, as it's my preferred position when I'm behind the wheel of most motors.

There's nothing I like more than slinging a car's rear end out of shape while being in full control at the helm – it makes me smile. And I feel so lucky to have done just that in thousands of vehicles over the years during my time as a road tester for various motoring magazines and as a presenter for BBC's *Top Gear* and Five's *Fifth Gear*.

And it's been fantastic to sort through my top 100 cars for this, my first book, and to remember some of the wonderful drives I've had, as well as some of the most disappointing.

My love of driving started as a toddler sitting on my father's knee as he drove tractors on his hard-working farm. As soon as I was tall enough to reach the pedals and steer, I did. And then I grabbed whatever vehicles I could to drive over the harvested fields every summer until I turned 12 and became old enough to start racing.

My father, Guy B-H, had raced karts for his country when he was a teenager and brushed down one of his old outfits for me to drive up and down the farm roads on, with a durable lawn-mower engine attached.

After a visit to our nearest kart racing track, Rye House at Hoddesdon in Hertfordshire, I caught the bug big time and pestered poor Dad so much he caved in and bought a modern racing kart with a two-stroke 100cc engine and we started racing.

My first race will always be memorable for me because one of my rivals was a certain David Coulthard, who went on to become one of Britain's most successful Formula One drivers. It wasn't his first race so I don't feel too ashamed to say he lapped me.

From then on I raced karts almost every weekend around the UK until I turned 17, when I progressed to race cars. At this stage I wanted to be a Formula One driver, but you need a lot of ingredients to come together at the right time to become one of the 20 or so drivers in the world – talent, money and luck – and it didn't work out for me. But I see that as a blessing because it made me turn my attention to becoming a journalist, writing about cars on and off the track.

This book captures many of those adventures and I really hope you enjoy reading about them as much as I had recalling them – which is a lot!

Vicki Butler-Henderson, London, 2010

100. JAGUAR XK8

99. JAGUAR XKR

98. HUMMER

97. HON

96

A FCX CLARITY

FORD MUSTANG

95. CHRYSLER VIPER

94. DODGE CHARGER

93. FORD GRAN TORINO

92. ASTON MARTIN DB7

91. AUDI TT

100. JAGUAR XK8
99. JAGUAR XKR

Jaguar's XK8 convertible is a car I'll never be able to forget. Unfortunately, for none of the right reasons. It was launched in the mid-1990s and I was with a bunch of British journalists who were invited to test the car on a road route through France. The weather was glorious, the roof remained down and the empty country roads were the perfect place to stretch the legs of the 4.0-litre V8. So far, so good.

ABOVE: This car put me off oysters for life. Its super smooth body is in stark contrast to the chunky flanks of the modern XKR (page 13) which has yet to give me a food allergy.

We stopped overnight at a hotel for the evening meal and very soon afterwards I doubled up with food poisoning, thanks to one tiny little cooked oyster. I have never been so violently ill. I can't eat the shellfish anymore, which is really sad considering I used to eat them not just by the dozen but by dozens of bucket loads. I can't look at an oyster or a Jag XK8 convertible now without thinking of that dreadful night.

The XK8 was the replacement for the XJS, a car I like to think was owned by dapper rogues for some reason, and the two cars shared the same floorplan. Their shapes were very different, though and where the XJS had bold, straight lines to its body, the XK8 was full and bulging, and captured the essence of relaxed speed. It was graceful, stylish and very much a British sports car.

Under that undulating bonnet was Jaguar's very first V8 engine, made from aluminium at a development cost of around £200 million. It was mated to an all-new five-speed automatic gearbox with a lever that went through a distinctive J-pattern gate between the front seats. There was no manual option.

A high level of technology went into the XK8 including the suspension, part of which was actually X-rayed for imperfections before it left the factory. The results were that the XK8 had a super-smooth ride, but also firmed up when you wanted to test its mettle as a sports car on demanding roads.

Jaguar was owned by Ford at the time and the emphasis was very much on making this car ooze Britishness. The interior options included plush and opulent leather and wood throughout, as well as a half-cow half-tree steering wheel which always seemed far too fussy to me. The company is currently owned by the Indian car maker Tata and the XK8 is in its second generation, alongside the hardcore sporty version, the XKR, which comes with those traditional interior trimmings still, or with snazzy aluminium.

A supercharger is bolted to the much bigger 5.0-litre V8, producing 510bhp that can hit 60mph in 4.6 seconds, which the driver can translate as "hit the gas and hang on". I drove one around Silverstone racing circuit for the *Sunday Times*, and even though the weather was awful and the track was like a swimming pool, the XKR growled and whined between corners with aggressive athleticism. The back end was snaking in a straight line as the tyres tried to gain traction. I kept my foot in and grabbed third and fourth gear from the paddle-shift controls of the six-speed auto box and foolishly went way over 100mph down the back straight. It was hairy stuff in such conditions, but I came away thinking Jag had managed to make a dominant sports car with the Olde English charms of a luxurious grand tourer.

"It was a graceful, stylish and very much British sports car."

THE FACTS

Engine: 4.0-litre V8 (XK8),
5.0-litre V8 supercharged (XKR)

Performance: 0–60mph in 5.2 seconds,
154mph (XK8),
0–60mph in 4.6 seconds,
155mph (XKR)

Price: £58,995 (XK8), £75,500 (XKR)

98. HUMMER

As soon as I saw one of these bulldoze its way down a British high street, I wanted one. Nobody, not even my car-loving mates, could understand the draw I felt toward them, but I just loved the fact they were so big, brash, bold and brutish.

I was filming for *Fifth Gear* at the Ace Café in London (a popular hang-out for petrol heads over the decades) and was waiting excitedly for an imported Hummer H2 to roll into the car park for me to test. It eventually rumbled into view and there was no getting away from the fact that it had a monster's presence.

It's little more than an American truck with an oblong body slapped on top and sprinkled with some flashy chrome. As aerodynamic as a block of flats, it has the elegance of one too. If you love sweeping arches and discrete bonnet bulges then this is not the car for you.

You need the skills of a mountain goat to climb on board and once you're in, its utilitarian interior is a long way from the sophistication afforded to Land Rover Discovery owners and the Hummer's interior height isn't as generous either. That was the biggest shock actually, considering it stands around two metres tall. Nothing could wilt my grin though as I fired up the 6.2-litre V8 and headed onto the nearest dual carriageway to wind my way through North London.

People had a good gawp at the Hummer as it rolled by and even if some were thinking how over-the-top it was, the machine's (I can hardly call it a car) rufty-tufty bodywork made me immune to them. It made me feel invincible, as if I was protected by some sort of life-proof casing. The windscreen was the car's most surprising feature, though, because it was about as deep as the mouth on a Post Office pillar box. Claustrophobia sufferers beware.

Although I didn't need its commendable off-road abilities during my urban test, I do know that it'll clamber over boulders and drive through streams, thanks to ground clearance of almost ten inches, short overhangs at each end and its four-wheel-drive set-up. We also filmed the smaller Hummer H3 for *Fifth Gear* and it managed the ascent along Welsh mountains without losing traction. Hummer's owner, GM, has now pulled the plug on the brand but its prehistoric looks and ways appealed to my quirky side while it was here.

LEFT: Just as leg warmers and ra-ra skirts were fashionable for the briefest period of time, so was the Hummer. David Beckham's environmental conscience wouldn't dare let him buy one now.

THE FACTS

Engine: 6.2-litre V8

Performance: 0–60mph in 8 seconds, 99mph (factory limited)

Price: $140,796

97. HONDA FCX CLARITY

This car is the only one of two in my top 100 that do not run on petrol so you might think it's an odd inclusion, but I think its fuel source is the one we could all be using in the future: hydrogen. The Honda FCX Clarity is the world's first hydrogen-powered production car and Honda should be heavily applauded for being the first manufacturer to put its money where its mouth is and invest heavily in this technology. The American state of California, led by the progressive Arnold Schwarzenegger, has given its full backing to the FCX Clarity. Its residents are currently able to lease 200 of them for the duration of a three-year programme. The actress Jamie Lee Curtis was one of the first to take delivery.

"It has a miles-per-gallon equivalent to 81mpg and can travel for 270 miles between fill-ups ..."

The sunshine state has invested in hydrogen filling stations and Honda is hoping the rest of the world will follow before it expands production of this super-green car and makes it available to the masses. At the moment the only hydrogen stations in the UK belong to a few universities, which they use to fuel various student projects but nothing on a large scale. The infrastructure just isn't in place yet for more manufacturers to justify their investment in hydrogen power. In the mid-2000s, BMW also ran a small fleet of seven-series luxury cars and there was a fleet of London buses that ran on it as well, though they were more promotional exercises than permanent commitments.

Honda's eco-hero is driven by a 100kw electric motor that turns the front wheels, so it is just like an electric car in that respect. But it's how the car powers that electric motor which is the unusual bit. Instead of pumping unleaded petrol into the fuel tank, hydrogen is pumped into the tank in exactly the same way as we fill our normal cars at a pump forecourt. That hydrogen is then mixed with oxygen from the atmosphere in a special unit called a fuel cell stack that sits hidden from view between the two front seats and is full of clever technology.

The electrochemical reaction that takes place in that fuel cell stack creates electricity that powers the 100kw electric motor, which then goes on to make the car move. If we were all paying attention in our school chemistry lessons, we should know that when you mix oxygen with hydrogen the end product is H_2O – water. So there are no carbon dioxides coming out of the Clarity, just water that you can sometimes see as steam. In California, Honda has designed it so that solar energy is used to create the hydrogen supply in the first place so its fuel is as green as can be.

It has a miles-per-gallon equivalent to 81mpg and can travel for 270 miles between fill-ups – a much more useful range than the current 40–80 miles achieved by the current crop of electric cars. The Honda will also carry four people and as much luggage as you'd get in a Renault Megane. It's not so accomplished to drive as a BMW 3-series, but the acceleration is decent enough for you to keep up with main traffic on every type of road and it handles as well as an average front-wheel-drive car. I think it's terrific and that it's got a great future.

LEFT: Cheryl Cole would never let her hair look so dank in a published photo...
It was raining hard whilst filming this car in Frankfurt, and I didn't have a brolly.

THE FACTS

Engine: 100kw electric motor

Performance: 0–60mph in 10 seconds, 100mph

Price: $600 dollars per month rental (£400 approx)

96. FORD MUSTANG

You can't walk past a Ford Mustang without noticing it, such is its road presence. It doesn't matter which model or how old it is. In 1964 the Mustang made its debut at New York's World Fair on April 17. It was the original "pony" car – a name Americans gave to all cars with long bonnets and short rear ends (sports coupés) such as the English Ford Capri.

"Like the devil has crept up on you to unleash a hellish scream in your ear ..."

The car still enjoys success today with the latest version, introduced in 2005. Though built in America, its popularity in the UK has created a growing business and steady revenue stream for many importers, as well as providing a great starting block for the modifying market. One such company is American-based UBB, Ultimate Bad Boy, which is run by a Brit, and which gave me the keys to the most powerful road car I've ever driven.

Before I reveal the astonishing number of horses, I need to put it into perspective. A normal family road car like a 2.0-litre Ford Mondeo has 143bhp. A sports car like Porsche's Boxster has 252bhp. A Ferrari F430 supercar has 483bhp and a Formula One car has around 800bhp, but this Mustang has more.

One thousand brake horsepower is the actual figure that UBB managed to squeeze out of the 5.4-litre V8. It has one of the biggest superchargers fitted to it that you'll find outside the drag racing world. It'll hit 60mph in 3.8 seconds and has a huge amount of torque, 825lb/ft – almost twice that of a Lamborghini Murcielago.

The UBB Mustang is an imposing sight with its orange paint job, black stripes and go-faster stickers, but that's nothing compared to the shivers it sends up your spine when you turn the ignition key and press the go button. It's like the devil has crept up on you to unleash a hellish scream in your ear at point-blank range. Its volume can increase to such a high level – 124 decibels, in fact – that permanent hearing loss is a real risk. Which is why, after a mere eight minutes at the wheel, I reached for some ear defenders.

Its 18-inch tyres are little more than legal cut-slicks and would be more at home on a racing circuit, but at least they stick to the tarmac as much as is physically possible. That's really reassuring

when you've got 1,000bhp demanding to be unleashed.

I hit the throttle hard from a standstill and the rear end squatted down with a jolt before it started to swing sideways as too much power failed to gain traction. The revs rose to 6,000rpm in first gear and still there was little forward progress so I snatched second gear and with a deafening roar that could be heard in the next county, we were finally off. And then it became the quickest accelerating car I've experienced – to think there's room in here for your family!

I buried the throttle once more in second and third gear, and felt the ferocity of the V8 suck out my soul and spit it onto the verge passing at gunfire rapidity. Once I'd remembered to breathe, I tried to stop swearing as the power, force and vibrations jolted through me. It was nerve-rackingly brilliant, like being on 10 roller coasters at once, and without doubt the trip of a lifetime in a road-legal car.

THE FACTS

Engine: 5.4-litre V8

Performance: 0–60mph in 3.8 seconds, 200mph +

Price: £78,000

LEFT: It's even brighter in the flesh – as is my turquoise jacket. What a beast. Car's not bad either.

95. CHRYSLER VIPER

When I think of Chrysler, the first motor that pops into my head is its overweight people carrier, the Voyager, which certainly hasn't made my top 100. The American-born company now has an alliance with the Italian car giant Fiat, but back in 1993 Chrysler made a car that appealed to me big time – the Viper was a muscle car made to give a supercar a run for its money. It was big, measuring more than 6 ft across, but Chrysler's clever engineers managed to keep the car's weight down to just over 1500kg, which is a similar weight to a Ford Focus.

The first time I realized it was perhaps a bit too wide for small European country roads was when I met a Mini flying into my path as I hurled round a bend toward it. Fortunately there was a grass verge for me to swoop onto, but it was a hairy moment, made a little more stressful by the fact that the Viper was left-hand-drive only. I had a great view of the hedge whizzing by me, though. There were many more cases of almost rubbing door handles with passing cars, but once the road opened up, the Viper lived up to its name.

Giving it 400bhp of venom was an 8.0-litre V10 engine that made this beast as rapid as a bite from a snake. In 4.3 seconds, it could hit 60mph from a standstill and keep on going to over 140mph. Its speed was of course aided by the two optional white "go-faster" stripes that could be fitted to the length of the car. Despite the impressive performance figures, it was actually wonderfully relaxing to drive. A strict two-seater, the seats were big and fat enough to fit a small family in each one, yet they were still perfectly shaped to hold just one person in place.

The six-speed manual gearlever needed a bit of muscle to shift it through the box, but once it was in, you could bury the throttle again and feel the car sit down on its 17-inch tyres and gallop onto the next one. Grip was in abundance, boosting its cornering capabilities, as did its suspension, which managed to be firm but still comfortable.

The car's design was certainly curvy and it attracted attention and smiles from all ages wherever we went. There were a couple of

LEFT AND ABOVE: If you want a dramatic entrance wherever you go, this is the perfect chariot: big, brash and noisy. Fabulous.

downsides to it, though, notably its bulges made it a bit difficult to see out of, especially if height isn't on your side. This became more of a issue when the fiddly roof was in place.

Then there was the fuel consumption. High enough to make Shell shareholders rub their hands in delight, it managed an average of around just 15mpg – meaning there must be some very low mpg numbers in that equation somewhere. Its boot wasn't a significantly size either. Practicality wasn't this car's main selling point – big grins were.

"Once the road opened up, the Viper lived up to its name."

THE FACTS

Engine: 8.0-litre V10

Performance: 0–60 mph in 4.6 seconds, 146mph

Price: £55,000

94. DODGE CHARGER
93. FORD GRAN TORINO

For me, these two cars are the epitome of American motors; I grew up watching them star in their separate US-imported TV series every week. The tomato-coloured 1974 Gran Torino belonged to the police pair of *Starsky and Hutch*. They may have rooted out the baddies, but I'm not sure how they stayed undercover with those conspicuous bright white stripes running almost the length of both sides. As you'd expect from the Yank tanks, it's big – it's 17ft 6 inches long, and it weighs two and a half tonnes. Under that vast bonnet is a 5.8-litre V8 engine, but it had "only" 250bhp to make it shift so it was hardly the quickest baddie-catcher in town.

" ... it nudged 100mph – but it felt like the slowest 100mph I've ever experienced."

Which is perhaps where the other of my favourites scores. The 1969 Dodge Charger RT sounded fast and was better-known as the General Lee from the TV show, *The Dukes of Hazard*. On its roof was the American Confederate Flag and the car took its name from an American Civil War leader. Although a few years older than the Gran Torino, its whopping 7.2-litre V8 engine produced more power, 375bhp, and it was a little lighter – although still on the porky side – at two-and-a-quarter tonnes. It was also a bit longer at 18 feet and was six feet wide. Huge.

Another astonishing fact was that this was a race car. As such, its doors were welded shut as part of the safety system – and so Luke, Bo and Daisy Duke had to slide in through the window each time in the show. It's the absolute opposite of the pert, lightweight racing cars that we know today, but then American circuits are generally wider than those in Europe, with fewer tight bends, which must have better suited the General Lee.

However, I was at a racing circuit in the UK when I got to put these two head to head. My mission was to find out which one was the quickest over a lap of the part-twisty and part-banked 1.9 mile -circuit at Rockingham.

Charging in the Charger, along the fastest part of the track, it nudged 100mph – but it felt the slowest 100mph I've ever experienced. As I tried to brake for the first tight right-hand bend not a lot happened, so perhaps it's just as well the speedo was on the optimistic side. Everything was in slow motion and the bends seemed to go on forever, no matter how slight they were. There was zero urgency from the car, which made it very relaxing to drive – so much so, actually, that I was cornering with one hand on the wheel and the other one playing the *Dukes of Hazard* theme tune on the horn. Da da da da da-da. Da da da da da-da!

The overall experience was quite similar when I tried to hustle the Gran Torino around next. It felt as though it was equally "quick" round the corners, but the bodywork almost bent down to kiss the tarmac. It wasn't as fast in a straight line, but the brakes were much more reassuring because they actually worked. Against the stop-watch, the Gran Torino crossed the finish line in two minutes 34.5 seconds, with the General Lee quicker by one and half seconds. It's got Number One on its door for a reason and I've never had so much fun going so slowly.

LEFT: Apologies for my very poor effort to emulate the delicious Daisy Duke from the 1980s TV show. Both her brother's car and the Gran Torino (**RIGHT**) were two of the most memorable motors I've driven because of their length and lack of speed.

THE FACTS

Engine: 5.8-litre V8 Gran Torino, 7.2-litre V8 Dodge Charger

Performance: 0–60 mph leisurely

Price: £priceless

92. ASTON MARTIN DB7

Aston Martin's DB7 is a car that has a unique place in my heart, but sadly not for joyous reasons. It holds the VBH crown for being the most disappointing car I've ever driven, which is pretty good going considering I've driven Rover's MGF... I can hear you screaming now that I must be a total buffoon to make such a bold claim - "the MGF isn't that bad, surely" you mutter, but just wait because it has its own special page later on. But back to the Aston and I know it looks divine, svelte and sophisticated, but looks can so easily deceive.

The DB7 was launched in 1994 and had the weight of the company on its roof. Success would have enabled them to enjoy one of the most profitable periods in their then 75-year history, whereas failure would probably have forced the parent company, Ford, to fold the luxury sports car arm.

History tells us the former proved to be the case, as the car went on to become the company's highest production model. More than 7,000 found homes across the world between 1993 and 2004, before it was replaced by the DB9, launched in 2003.

On paper, and in pictures, I absolutely fell in love with the DB7. It lit my fuse on all counts from its chassis – rear-wheel-drive – to its engine, a 3.2-litre, 335bhp engine that had more power and torque than Aston's bigger 5.3-litre V8 unit. Mostly, it managed that thanks to a supercharger that made sure it delivered its goods as soon as throttle demanded, without any hint of delay.

As with most superchargers, it whines as it works and so gives the DB7 a slightly unusual voice. But even that didn't put me off. And then Aston unveiled a topless version, the Volante, and its slender profile stopped me in my tracks. It had gone beyond beautiful and I had utterly fallen under its spell: I *had* to drive it.

Which is when my dreams shattered. Wise men say you should never meet your hero because they're unlikely to reach the pedestal you've put them on. I should have listened.

From the moment the key entered my hand, I felt let down. Duped, even, because it resembled a Ford Mondeo key. Adding insult to this increasingly painful injury was the interior – full to bursting with Ford switches, buttons, dials, air vents ... I appreciate economics meant sharing the parts bin, but when you're paying almost £80,000 for a car you want to be pushing platinum, not plastic.

With the smile on my face heading downward, I fired up the engine and went for first gear. Another punch of disappointment hit home as the gear lever needed the force of two arms to shove it through the five-speed gate. The steering lacked the finesse you need to take such a fast car through its paces. It all felt as though it had been hurried out of the factory having missed out on those vital finishing touches. I never even managed to get fully comfortable behind the wheel either – and that is a rare thing for me.

All these years later it's astonishing that the DB7 still retains the unwanted crown I gave it, but perhaps it made me lower my expectations for other cars, and so it will always keep its place. I've included it in my top 100 because, despite a broken heart, the DB7 is still desirable. Just don't open the door.

LEFT: This DB7 should make my pulse quicken – it looks great, has a wonderful heritage and is the brand of choice for James Bond - but it has the opposite effect. My tears continue.

" ... the DB7 is still desirable. Just don't open the door."

THE FACTS

Engine: 3.2-litre 6-cylinder

Performance: 0–60 mph in 5.6 seconds, 157mph

Price: £78,500

91. AUDI TT

Audi's TT Roadster had such feminine looks when it was launched in 1999 that I felt obliged to wear a skirt and some Gucci heels when I tested it for BBC's *Top Gear*. I ditched the stilettos as soon as I sat in it, though – I have no idea how it's physically possible to drive in them. But better women than me do, and they look good.

ABOVE: The Roadster has been a big hit with stylish women who appreciate the luxury and quality that's overflowing in Audi's two-seater. Men favour the more practical coupé version.

" ... it remains an aspirational car for many professional girlfriends of mine."

The two-seater soft-top followed quickly in the tyre tracks of the Coupe TT, the car considered more practical because of its two rear seats that could fit a couple of youngsters – or a good haul of shoes.

It looked a little like a squashed and elongated Volkswagen Beetle, but actually had more in common with the Golf and A3, sharing the same platform. The TT was on sale with either a front-wheel-drive chassis, which most cars on the road have, or with the quattro "on demand" system, much valued by people in need of some extra reassurance round corners or in poor weather. This car was, and still is very much a statement vehicle, but you don't have to break the bank for it. Tens of thousands of style-conscious drivers have bought into its image and it remains an aspirational car for many professional girlfriends of mine.

Now, much as I appreciate a gorgeous piece of metal, I'm not the kind of girl who cares massively about a car's looks. My reasoning being that I'll spend most of the time actually driving, so the important bits are the chassis and engine. However, Audi designers have grabbed my attention with *their* attention inside the TT, which includes visual delights such as baseball-stitched leather seats in the Roadster, or Recaro race seats and a brace in the quattro Sport.

Of all the mass-producing manufacturers, Audi knows how to spoil its passengers with perfectly placed and wonderfully weighted buttons and switches. Quality materials are sprinkled with glitzy trimmings that make you wonder why a girl needs diamonds when she could have all this.

Its fashionable interior is well matched with impeccable road manners and I think it's the most polite car I've driven. No matter what type of road you're on or what speed you're at, the TT will do everything brilliantly. The only fault is a tendency to under-steer in protest if you're too greedy with the power in a bend. Now, I know this is going to seem irrational to some people, but it is precisely this Headgirl behaviour that stops me from truly loving the TT. I'm more drawn to the down-and-dirty antics that the rear-wheel-drive Nissan 350Z offers, but they run each other very close.

In 2006, the second generation TT emerged and it's available with an engine to suit most demands, from a turbocharged diesel to the all-singing 3.2-litre V6 with a six-speed gearbox and steering-mounted paddle shift levers. There's still a manual for the old-school among us, though I tested both gearboxes for *Fifth Gear* at Rockingham racing circuit to see which was quickest over a lap. The super-quick shifts of the S-tronic won by just four-tenths of a second.

THE FACTS

Engine: 1.8-litre four-cylinder to 3.2-litre V6

Performance: 0–60 mph in 7.2 seconds to 4.8 seconds, 140mph +

Price: £26,245 +

90. TESLA

89. ROLLS-ROYCE

88. MASERA

87. FIAT

86.

PHANTOM

TI QUATTROPORTE

500

TROFEO ABARTH 500 GB RACER

85. FORD CAPRI

84. LAND ROVER DEFENDER

83. LAND ROVER RANGE ROVER

82. ALFA ROMEO SZ

81. ALFA ROMEO RZ

90. TESLA

The Tesla is the world's first electric-powered supercar. It can hit 60mph from a standstill in 3.9 seconds and is without a doubt the quietest car I've ever driven in anger. I tested it at the Goodwood Festival of Speed in 2008, where its silence stunned me to a similar state, especially when surrounded by cars that made some of the best sounds in the world.

E ach year the star-studded and car-packed event sees some of the best road, rally and track cars blast up the 1.16-mile long hill route against the clock, weaving their way past the sensational Goodwood stately home. The drivers show off each car's talents to the thousands of enthusiastic fans lining the way and everyone is eager to see which car is the fastest. Its driver then gets bragging rights at the glamorous evening party afterwards.

The two-seater Tesla is based on the Lotus Elise and so it at least looks the part of a fast car. It would have won the "I didn't hear you coming" award, had there been one, particularly as my run up the hill followed a flame-breathing, petrol-pumping, ear-splitting V8 racer. I was suited, booted and gloved like I was about to wrestle a Nascar but I had to make my own "brrrm, brrrm" noises as I crept up to the start line.

"The only thing I could hear through my helmet was the wind whistling over the top of the windscreen."

With an electric motor the maximum amount of torque is available pretty much all the time you're moving forward, which for this car meant I could use all its grunt from zero revs all the way through to its 13,000rpm limit. There is only one gear (and a reverse) so I popped the gearlever into the "go" position and was ready to hit the throttle to dictate my speed.

I booted it off the line and there was enough torque to push me back a bit into my seat, even if there was no noise to accompany such thrust. I accelerated up to around 90mph on the fastest part of the course and the Tesla really did feel quick but it just didn't sound it. The only thing I could hear through my helmet was the wind whistling over the top of the windscreen.

As I slowed for the biggest 90-degree left-hand bend I realized how much I subconsciously rely on noise to gauge my speed, but because there was no drop in engine noise here, or a change in gear which you'd even get in an automatic, I wasn't sure if my new speed was good enough to get quickly round the corner. I couldn't get any of this information from listening to the Tesla and I found that disconcerting. I'll never again think of a car's noise as simply a sexy by-product.

At the end of the run the Tesla Roadster had seriously impressed me even though we weren't the fastest of the day. With its range of 220 miles between charges too, it showed that electric cars don't all need to be dull city dwellers.

ABOVE AND RIGHT: I had never driven so quickly so quietly until I met the Tesla. Finally, a poster-car for the plug-in generation.

THE FACTS

Engine: Electric

Performance: 0–60mph in 3.9 seconds, 100mph+

Price: £75,000

89. ROLLS-ROYCE PHANTOM

I don't know how it manages it, but every time a Rolls-Royce Phantom drives past me it does so in utter silence. And what's even more puzzling is that it's one of the biggest cars in the world at 20-feet long and is powered by a great big V12 engine.

"As wide as a palace, the car's girth proved a bit too much for some of the narrow country lanes ... "

Owned by the German manufacturer BMW, the Rolls-Royce Phantom still epitomizes all that's English and it's made at a purpose-built, state-of-the-art factory at Goodwood near Chichester in West Sussex too – a very picturesque part of England steeped in motorsport history. I went to Rolls-Royce's HQ in 2003 to test the then-new Phantom and before I was given the keys, I had a behind-the-scenes tour to see how a quarter of a million pounds is put together. Carefully, I'd say.

It's a huge place with a lot of natural light to encourage creativity, and there are specific departments that look after each segment of the building process. There's a place where the leather is dyed and one where it gets stitched together, another for the carving and polishing of the wood interior and again another which houses a special machine to hydraulically raise an almost-finished car and then shake it about to test the air springs.

The Phantom's ride quality is one of the most important features because everyone expects a Rolls-Royce to majestically transport its occupants in world-class comfort as though they are floating on the fibres of the deepest and softest carpet. Phantoms are definitely geared more toward pampering the passengers than the chauffeur up front, but when you get behind the wheel, you feel like royalty surrounded with the beautiful results of so many people's hard work, finished with painstaking precision. The whole place shines like it's ready for a state banquet. It's also as eerily quiet inside as it is when I'm standing outside one, such is the amazing sound-insulation throughout the car.

As wide as a palace, the car's girth proved a bit too much for some of the narrow country lanes surrounding Goodwood, so

I was forced to slacken the pace and let the V12 trickle along at low revs. Which it did admirably. When the road eventually opened up, the rear-drive chassis planted the engine's 453bhp eagerly and we galloped gracefully along.

Head for the back seat, and you have to open the solid doors (or have staff to do this for you), which open outward from the middle of the car. Then you step up and into the most luxurious room you'll ever see on four wheels, with more polish and cowhide than seems possible. It's so decadent back here that it would not be foolish for you to expect fully-catered afternoon tea to be offered. Just think: its 6.8-litre V12 still manages to shift this two-and-a-half tonnes penthouse apartment to 60mph in 5.7 seconds – that's quicker than a Porsche Boxster.

THE FACTS

Engine: 6.8-litre V12

Performance: 0–60mph in 5.7 seconds, 149mph

Price: £275,990

LEFT: Looking at this car is like looking at the Mona Lisa as it's a breath-taking piece of art. It gets even better when you step inside (the similarities to Mona Lisa stop here I think).

88. MASERATI QUATTROPORTE

I can't imagine any other car manufacturer calling its luxury saloon car "Four Doors", but that's exactly what Maserati did in the 1960s. The company was clever enough to use the Italian word *Quattroporte*, though, which instantly makes the phrase sound exceptionally exotic. The top-end lavish motor has had many incarnations since then, and today, as well as its number of doors, there are three metallic-surrounded vents just behind the front wheel arches. To me, they look like the equivalent of the diamond earrings that finish off a glamorous outfit.

"... the Trident badge on one of the most recognizable grilles in the motoring world ... guarantees you entry everywhere."

The Quattroporte is so stylish and elegant that just one look is enough to transport your thoughts to Monaco, St Tropez or Biarritz, and a host of exquisite social gatherings. But none more so – in my mind anyway – than my wedding, when I was taken to the church in the back of a Quattroporte. It was one of the most exciting one-mile journeys I've ever had because my racing-driver brother was at the helm. Just like me – again, in my mind at least – the Quattroporte is a thoroughbred that doesn't come cheap.

It works well as a chauffeur's car, with hand-stitched leather in the back to cosset the most demanding derrière, and of course with that Trident badge on one of the most recognizable grilles in the motoring world, it guarantees you entry everywhere. Rivals include BMW's 7-series, Mercedes-Benz's S-Class and Audi's R8. While all three are more of a complete package, the Maserati's unique character pulls hardest at your heart strings.

Tugging hardest of all is the sound of the 4.7-litre V8 fitted to the Quattroporte's two-car line-up, though the £85,000 S has 425bhp and the near-£92,000 GT S has 433bhp. The bark it delivers on start-up is enough to remind you that all that money has been very well spent. It'll go on to hang onto the revs in all six gears to leave your ears ringing with rich Italian notes all day. In comparison, its rivals are more grown-up and muted.

ABOVE: On the short journey to my wedding my brother Charlie matched this car's 0–62mph, and much as I tried to tell him off, I loved every one of the 5.4 seconds.

It's not slow off the mark, with a 0–62mph time of 5.4 seconds and a top speed in excess of 170mph, but maintain such a heavy right foot and you'll pay for it with a fuel-economy figure hovering in the mid-teens. But if you run a Quattroporte, life will be too good to worry about such trivia. That's the main essence of this car – its grace grabs you and never lets go, and despite its flaws it is the only sporting saloon that offers something wonderfully different to the safe options from Germany. It's a passionate car for passionate people.

THE FACTS

Engine: 4.7-litre V8

Performance: 0–62mph in 5.4 seconds, 174mph

Price: £85,005

87. FIAT 500

86. TROFEO ABARTH 500 GB RACER

In the early part of the new millennium, BMW's revitalized Mini recaptured the fun of motoring with its chic and classy-looking city car. A modern version of the classic 1960s "it" car, it had been cleverly revamped and repackaged, and most importantly, was in a class of its own. Until Fiat jumped onto the retro bandwagon and re-launched its former icon, the 500, that is. At last there was an alternative to the Mini and the Fiat offered just as much in the way of stylish looks, quirky colours and trim patterns, and was dripping with cuteness to make it another must-have motoring accessory.

"... 500s are seriously jolly to drive and make the perfect companion for the school run ..."

The engine line-up varies from a 1.2-litre 68bhp to the scorching 1.4-litre turbocharged Abarth model with 157bhp, so there's something to suit most lifestyles. There are two choices of roof, too: a hard- or a soft-top. No matter which you go for, or what colour scheme you pick, the 500s are seriously jolly to drive and make the perfect companion for the school run, a shopping trip or lunch at the swankiest restaurant. Admittedly the 500 doesn't have the crisp handling of the Mini, but it's a lot kinder on the wallet – the entry-level model, for example, is almost £5,000 cheaper than Mini's base car. That's a lot of handbags.

The hottest version of the car, the Abarth 500, also has a new one-make racing series to complement its range and boost brand awareness. Called the Trofeo Abarth 500 GB, it's for identical race-prepared Abarth 500s that compete in 14 races at circuits throughout the year. I'm very proud to say that my younger brother Charlie, who's been racing since he was 8 years old, is competing in the series. He finished second in the first-ever race at Oulton Park at the start of 2010.

I pulled rank on him – as is a big sister's privilege – to test the car before him pre-season and thought it was not only a hoot to drive, but also a big handful, if doing so quickly. The car has a really short wheelbase (the length between the front and rear axle) and a tall body – an unusual combination for a racing car.

It's powered by the hot 1.4-litre turbo unit that's been tweaked to produce 190bhp, and it has more torque than a 2.0-litre Audi TT. It races on 17-inch slick tyres in the dry and specially-cut grooved ones in the wet, and it's also fitted with a front and rear spoiler to make it stick to the tarmac and make it as fast as possible. The racing car is not a million miles away from the street-legal Abarth 500 inside. It still has the large circular speedo, dashboard, heater dials and even the electric window mechanisms – very decadent in a racer.

"… guaranteed fun."

The six-speed gearbox is from Fiat's Grande Punto SS road car and it's not the quickest when it comes to race-pace changes. This also means the drivers can't be as rough with it as a more motorsport-focused box, but at least that gives their brains something to think about as well as their muscles. The AP Racing brakes don't have the luxury of an anti-lock system (unlike the road cars) so a sensitive foot is the only way to avoid tyre-smoking lock-ups at the end of a straight. Whether you drive a Trofeo racer or a Fiat 500, though, one thing you're guaranteed is fun.

LEFT/RIGHT: How dull the city car market would be without this cheeky little Italian – and how versatile it is with its own racing series for the hottest Abarth versions.

THE FACTS

Engine: from 1.2-litre four-cylinder to 1.4-litre turbocharged (500), 1.4-litre four-cylinder turbocharged (Trofeo)

Performance: 0–60mph from 12.5 seconds, 101mph (500), 0–60mph sub-7.0 seconds, 130mph+ (Trofeo)

Price: from £9,300 (500), £25,000 (Trofeo)

85. FORD CAPRI

Before I was old enough to drive one, I didn't have a particularly high opinion of Ford's Capri – or Crapi, as I've heard them called. I think their biggest problem was a poor image. Now, having driven many of them, I think they are one of the coolest cars ever to have graced our roads. They were named after the Isle of Capri, off the Italian coast, not too far from Naples, and launched as the UK's answer to America's user-friendly sports car, the Ford Mustang. The Capri was the car of choice not only for the TV spy show *"The Professionals"* but also for my fellow *Fifth Gear* presenter and racing driver Tiff Needell, who owned one in his time.

"The tyres smoked easily too, so my antics looked as good on the camera as if I was driving a supercar ..."

This is one of the best cars I've ever driven for teaching you about oversteer. It is tail-out-tastic and I wish it was still in production today. I would make every teenager drive one to learn the basic skills of car control. The Capri had no fancy gadgets or trick technology on it, just a simple rear-drive chassis and front-mounted engines, with absolutely no traction control systems. Hurrah! This means that even at low speeds, on an empty bit of tarmac, you can make the Capri dance and swing its tail about until you're either sick or you've travelled some way toward mastering the technique of holding the slides. Which is exactly what I did when I had the whole of Kemble Airfield, near Cirencester, to play on during a film day for *Fifth Gear*.

The car I drove was a 2.8 V6 Injection Special that was one of the last ones ever to be made and it was also in near-showroom condition. Built in 1986, it had had just one owner from new, who had barely driven 30,000 miles in it. It came with sought-after features like a five-speed manual gearbox (a given today), colour-coded door mirrors, original Recaro seats and even the same Ford stereo/cassette unit that was fitted at the factory.

The engine produced 157bhp, which is nowadays pretty standard for many motors, but with no driver aids its power could be a potent weapon in the right hands, i.e. mine. I had a great laugh getting the rear end to slide out one way and then the other

just by giving it a little dab of the throttle and a spin of the three-spoke steering wheel. The tyres smoked easily too, so my antics looked as good on-camera as if I was driving a supercar but for a fraction of that price at under £8,000 new. If only those prices could stay the same.

The Ford may not have the sumptuous body of an Aston Martin, but the Capri is definitely a GT car that gives you big bangs for small bucks. It just goes to show that first impressions can be very, very wrong.

LEFT: Some may think this is the ultimate Essex pin-up and I couldn't agree more. But it also transcends class barriers because it's such an iconic motor.

THE FACTS

Engine: 2.8-litre V6

Performance: 0–60mph in 7.9 seconds, 129mph

Price: £7,993

83. LAND ROVER RANGE ROVER
84. LAND ROVER DEFENDER

This side of a Union Flag there's not much that's more British than a Land Rover, especially the no-frills Defender, which seems to have been around since God created mud. The Series I was actually launched at the Amsterdam Motor Show in 1948 and was called a utility vehicle for a reason. It was a no-nonsense workhorse with zero cabin comfort that suited the military, farmers and anyone on a far-flung expedition. Hideously prehistoric compared to most off-roaders on sale today, it's noisy, bumpy and not at all relaxing to drive or be a passenger in. But that's the special appeal of the Defender and precisely why more than two million have found homes around the world.

"… I love climbing up into the driver's seat after a really long day …"

It wasn't until 1990 that the name Defender was created and it is still as agricultural in its design as when it was first unveiled. It could be taken apart with just a few tools, making it a great project for DIY enthusiasts and for the ever-popular band of off-road racers who spend competitive weekends plunging deep ravines in the name of sport. Land Rover owners relish the fact that other cars may be faster but theirs is the one that can go anywhere.

Defenders come in a variety of shapes, including short and long wheelbases, and with three or five doors. It's the descendants of the smallest original that I love the look of most, even though the latest one's 2.4-litre diesel engine hits 60mph in 14.7 seconds and has a top speed of just 82mph.

But the Land Rover I fell in love with so much that I bought one is the company's most opulent model, the Range Rover. This has almost as much mud-plugging ability as the Defender but it cossets its passengers in a comparatively-obscene amount of luxury. The seats are well-cushioned for starters and would be equally at home in your front room, and of course they are wrapped in the finest cow hide.

My father has had Ranger Rovers for most of his life, as they are fantastic for carrying bits and bobs of farm machinery over fields – or picnics, for that matter. I have the best memories of driving hundreds of lunches over to him as he worked in his combine harvester every summer and then sitting with him on the bottom half of the Range Rover's split tailgate, eating a sarnie and swinging our legs.

And it's almost entirely because of that "seat" that I recently bought a secondhand 4.4-litre V8 HSE Range Rover of my own. It may only do 18mpg at best, and I know some people hate them just for the sake of hating them, but I love climbing up into the driver's seat after a really long day. I can almost point it

toward home and it'll carry me there without effort. It's the first automatic I've ever owned too, but on these journeys I'm grateful to let my left leg rest.

During the years, I've seen Range Rovers emerge from the field and find their way onto the smartest forecourts to become a highly sought-after brand. Curiously, I'm not a fan of the most performance-oriented Sport versions as I think they are too urban for my traditional tastes and they're not as smooth when it comes to the ride quality, either. If everyone could experience the comfort, interior space and grace that other Range Rovers offer then I'm certain all those haters would disappear overnight.

LEFT: The RR is such an all-round delight that I parted with my own money and bought one. And I've been parting with more ever since, each time I fill the tank.

THE FACTS

Engine: 2.4-litre four-cylinder (Defender) from 3.0-litre V6 (Range Rover)

Performance: 0–60mph from 14.7 seconds, 82mph (Defender),0–60mph from 5.9 seconds to 8.8 seconds, from 120 to 140mph (Range Rover)

Price: from £23,170 (Defender); from £45,895 (Range Rover)

82. ALFA ROMEO SZ
81. ALFA ROMEO RZ

More than 10 years before I had the pleasure of testing Alfa Romeo's 8C supercar, I got my first taste of the manufacturer's smaller – but just as sexy – sports car. It's a proper little pocket rocket with all the character, charm and kudos you'd ever want from a car. If I'd had the cash to buy one, and insure it, it would have made my perfect first car.

"In total contrast to the cars' glamorous shapes and sparkling paintwork, we were shooting them in a wet and windy car park ... Oh, the glitz."

Called SZ in its hard-top form, this two-seater was also known as the RZ in convertible guise. The letters stand for Sprint Zagato and Roadster Zagato – Zagato being the Italian design house. They have a CV that includes creations for most of the Italian car industry, as well as Aston Martin, and Peugeot's 2010 offering, the RCZ. A big fascination for working with letters, clearly.

The SZ was launched in 1989, with the RZ later in 1992, so both had already been on sale for a good decade by the time I got my grubby little paws on them, filming the two models for an item on BBC's *Top Gear* show. In total contrast to the cars' glamorous shapes and sparkling paintwork, we were shooting them in a wet and windy car park at the front of a hotel in Guildford. Oh, the glitz.

The SZ was one of the most aerodynamic shapes of its time and although it may seem a bit angular for modern tastes, I think it's a stunning design. I still can't help but gawp whenever I see one, but that is rare, because just 1036 SZs and 284 RZs were ever built.

Underneath, its foundations came from Alfa's 75 racing car, which meant it was rear-wheel-drive. Perfect for a sports car. It was also relatively light at 1280kg, thanks to a plastic composite body, and that helped the 3.0-litre, 207bhp engine hit 62mph in seven seconds. Today, a similarly-powered six-cylinder BMW Z4 is just half a second quicker – the SZ was no slouch.

Slip into the leather-clad interior and you're faced with a dashboard unique to the car, especially as you could only buy it in left-hand drive guise. This wasn't too much of a hardship, though because Alfa Romeo cabins were created with the driver very much in mind. With the dash angled toward you, you feel an integral part of the whole car.

From this commanding position you can fully exploit that race car-like handling and the smooth power delivery from the V6. It may not be as quick or as agile round a circuit today as a BMW Z4, because sports cars have moved on, but the Alfa still has the magical ability to make you *seem* fast. Both the SZ or the RZ make every journey a bit special, though, because of the unusual looks, and that's a feat that many manufacturers aim for, but only a few achieve.

THE FACTS

Engine: 3.0-litre V6

Performance: 0–62 mph in 6.9 seconds, 152mph

Price: Italian Lira 93,044,000+ (c. £40,000+ in 1989)

LEFT: On June 24th 2010 Alfa Romeo celebrated its 100th birthday. When I'm 100, I hope to be thrashing around one of these gorgeous creations.

80. FERRARI 308 GTS

79. FORD RACING

78. FORD PUM

77. BMW

76.

UMA

A

Z8

BMW Z1

75. RENAULT ALPINE A610 TURBO

74. MERCEDES-BENZ SLS AMG

73. HOLDEN HSV

72. JAGUAR XJ220

71. MASERATI GRAN CABRIO

80. FERRARI 308 GTS

Ferrari's targa-top two-seater 308 found everlasting fame in the 1980s, thanks to a hairy-chested American man who ran around wielding a gun and some very short shorts. That man was Thomas Magnum, private investigator, who gave his name to the hit TV show. He was played by actor Tom Selleck, who was tall, dark and handsome and became my first crush. His Ferrari was my second.

ABOVE RIGHT: As much as I'd like to write an intelligent caption for this fabulous car, I am too busy drooling at the exquisite photo of my dream husband. Tom, Tom, Tom.

Actually, it wasn't his car. It belonged to his unseen writer boss, Robin Masters. That never seemed to be an issue, however, as Magnum drove like he'd stolen it most of the time. The 308 GTS – the hard-top version was badged GTB – looked as fast as Magnum himself, and even before it spun its rear wheels it was the perfect combination of man and machine – at least in my little eyes.

I don't think its sharp edges, pointed front end, clean lines and circular tail lights would look too out-of-place in showrooms today. Designed by famed styling house Pininfarina, it was launched at the 1975 Paris Motor Show and barely changed shape for more than a decade. It was Ferrari's replacement to the iconic Dino sports car and was thought of as a Ferrari for the masses. The company certainly got that right, because it was bought by almost 20,000 people around the world – with a particularly high number going to American owners who obviously bought into the Magnum image. They had a bigger passion for the GTS than the GTB, too.

If you've had the pleasure of watching some of the re-runs of the TV show, you'll know that fruity growl is the unmistakable voice of the car's 3.0-litre V8 engine, seated just ahead of the rear tyres. I was given the chance to emulate my hero when I drove a 308 for a *Fifth Gear* item along the seafront and streets of Brighton a few years ago, as well as stretching its legs on the winding country roads inland.

I felt like the cat with the cream as I cruised by busy cafés with the V8 burbling softly in my wake. People stared a lot, mostly because I was being followed by the camera crew but also, I hope because, like me, they were spellbound by this bright red Ferrari, the closest we'd all get to Tom Selleck.

In less-populated areas I unleashed the V8 to taste its 255bhp, and it was sweet. Even though the car was more than 20 years old, it gave me a sense of how easy it was to drive for its time, although the five-speed manual gearbox needed a precise throw to engage each gear. As I disappeared away from the camera's lens at the end of the day, my head filled with thoughts of being Mrs Magnum.

"I felt like the cat with the cream as I cruised by busy cafés with the V8..."

THE FACTS

Engine: 3.0-litre V8

Performance: 0–60 mph in 7.0 seconds, 146mph

Price: £15,499

78. FORD PUMA

79. FORD RACING PUMA

These may seem odd inclusions in my top 100 but if you've ever driven a Puma you'll know exactly how such a little car can generate so much entertainment. So much so in fact, that shortly after its launch in 1997, this three-door petite coupe was named BBC 2 *Top Gear*'s Car of the Year. No mean feat for a motor carrying the blue oval badge on its bonnet because this accolade has also been bestowed upon creations from Rolls-Royce Bugatti and Lamborghini. So the Puma can certainly punch above weight.

" ... I think its looks have stood the test of time pretty well."

For starters it looked fantastic, with its slick headlamps, bulbous wheel arches and slender middle, and I think its looks have withstood the test of time pretty well. Inside, it was equally fashionable with a well-designed but simple dashboard, white dials (as much a matter of personal taste then as they are now) and an aluminium gear lever that looked good but could freeze to your hand on a winter's morning. A clear case of style over substance there.

The five-speed gearbox was a peach and it came with a 1.4-litre petrol engine (later a 1.6-litre) and a range-topping 1.7-litre Zetec one, which gave a spritely 0–60mph time of 8.6 seconds and a top speed of 123mph. It wasn't the most powerful vehicle on the market by any stretch but it was very keen to rev and ever-willing to please, and it was almost as light as a Ford Ka is today so the power-to-weight ratio was at its optimum.

But the best thing about the Puma was its chassis. Based on the Ford Fiesta, the front-wheel-drive set-up was simply fantastic. The steering was a joy to turn and you could point it at a certain place in a corner and the 15-inch front tyres would hit the spot with a sniper's accuracy. There was a little roll from the body when cornering hard, but otherwise it stayed level to the road at the high speeds, the tyres fiercely gripped.

I remember testing one at a disused airfield when I worked as a Road Tester on a car magazine and was thrilled at how enjoyable it was when I indulged in a spot of lift-off oversteer. This is where you quickly pitch a front-wheel-drive car into a fast turn and then immediately lift off the throttle. This unbalances the car so much that, combined with the speed, it forces the back end to break traction and go sideways. Some timely turns of the steering and more power can have it sliding in the opposite direction, too and I could have done that all day long. It's such a good driver's car, even with the smallest engine.

It was easy to run as well because if anything went wrong there was a Ford dealer on almost every corner to sort it out. And with shared Fiesta parts, the Puma was a car that gave you sports car sensations without the big running costs. But if you were the sort of person who needed to have more of everything, then the Racing Puma would have been more your thing.

The Racing Puma was a limited run of just 500 hardcore Pumas that came in one colour, Ford's Racing Blue. Its wider wheel arches extended over 17-inch alloys to look like a steroid-pumped version of the original. The interior had Sparco bucket seats trimmed in blue pseudo-suede that did nothing to help cushion you from its rock-hard ride, but at least the potent 153bhp modified 1.7-litre engine more than made up for it.

ABOVE: Sometimes choice can be too much, so hats off to Ford, which offered its potent Racing Puma in blue only. Luckily for me it's my favourite colour.

THE FACTS

Engine: 1.4-litre, 1.6-litre and 1.7-litre four-cylinder (Puma), 1.7-litre four-cylinder (Racing Puma)

Performance: 0–60mph from 10.6 seconds to 8.6 seconds, from 111mph to 123mph (Puma), 0–60mph in N/A seconds, 140mph (Racing Puma)

Price: £13,200 – £14,550 £23,000 (Racing Puma)

77. BMW Z8

76. BMW Z1

In 1987, when big hair and faded denim filled the pavements, BMW launched a car that had such sharp looks it was even given a name that meant "future" (*Zukunft*). It was the first of the company's breed of two-seater roadsters and helped to slice a path which the Z8, Z3 and Z4 would eventually travel.

ABOVE: Some car lines deserve to be carried on, and that includes these two. The Z8 (above) looks better with no hard-top, but I wouldn't say no if one arrived on my drive.

The Z1's specially-developed rear-drive chassis supported an equally-special thermoplastic body that could be removed in panels and swapped for different coloured ones if the owner so wished. For me, its best party trick is the doors, which don't open upward or outward, but downward. The car's sills are very high – running alongside your thigh – giving good crash protection, and almost make the doors redundant in that respect. At the press of a button, the doors drop to expose more of the driver than you'd think possible. I'll never forget seeing a friend of mine unexpectedly pulling up alongside me in a Z1 at a set of traffic lights in London, dropping the car door to reveal a shocking pair of shorts. I wish more of them had been built – the car, not the shorts.

The roof could fold away as well, if its occupants wanted to experience a spot of open-air motoring. This was deemed enough for the Z1 not to offer air conditioning. Another reason for that decision was the dashboard was so small there wasn't enough space for the buttons, let alone the actual unit within the car.

Its eye-popping looks weren't backed by performance figures, though, with a 0–60mph time of 7.9 seconds and a top speed of 140mph. Its 2.5-litre six-cylinder engine had 170bhp, pretty asthmatic by today's standards, and it was sourced from BMW's 325i, along with its five-speed manual gearbox. It was big on fun, however, as was its showroom price – enough to have bought you the much-larger, luxurious 735i. But that didn't deter the 8,000 people who bought one.

In 1999, almost a decade after the death of the Z1, BMW had another foray into the two-seater topless market with its Z8 sports car. I was one of the first journalists to drive it when I tested the car for *Fifth Gear*. I travelled to America's sunny climes where it was built, to do so.

At the launch, BMW wanted to make sure the UK journalists found enough tight turns to emulate British roads and evaluate its handling, so we were sent to a very tight temporary track. The Z8 was fabulous – its big 5.0-litre V8 engine gave it enough power to slide its rear end addictively from one side to the other. That made it perfect for the quick-thrill seeker. But because the car was designed more for the US market, the overall characteristic was that it was an even better cruiser and therefore more comfortable than agile, so almost half of the near-6,000 that were made ended up staying in the States.

The thinking behind the Z8 was that it was a celebration of BMW's 507 car from the 1950s. Much of its styling is reminiscent of that car, though the Z8 was clearly deemed handsome enough to share the big screen with James Bond, as it made an appearance in *The World Is Not Enough*. It's earned its place in my Hot 100 by being a very enjoyable and perfectly proportioned muscle car.

"At the press of a button, the doors drop to expose more of the driver than you'd think possible."

THE FACTS

Engine: 2.5-litre six-cylinder (Z1), 5.0-litre V8 (Z8)

Torque: 493bhp (turbo model)

Performance: 0–60 mph in 7.9 seconds, 140mph (Z1); 0–60 mph in 4.7 seconds, 155mph (Z8)

Price: DM 83,000 (Z1), £80,000 (Z8)

75. RENAULT ALPINE A610 TURBO

There are a few cars which unfortunately slip under most people's radar for no obvious reasons or faults, and Renault's Alpine is one of them. Launched in the mid-1980s, it was Renault's answer to Porsche's 928 and as such was rear-engined, rear-wheel-drive and really great to drive. Its French looks included pop-up headlamps. They didn't give it quite the same pizazz as any one of Porsche's iconic designs, but I loved the Alpine and it was one of the first high-performance cars I ever drove in my teens.

ABOVE: I go weak at the knees when I even think about this car which is so bizarre because it's no Ferrari or Lamborghini. It deserved greater success than it achieved.

"... I see the odd one passing by once a year, if I'm lucky."

Admittedly it was an unconventional choice for anyone to spend money on, though I like to think it appealed to unconventional people who would appreciate features like its quirky interior door handles mounted in the cabin floor. Crazy, and all the better for it.

In early 1990 Renault brought out my absolute favourite version, the Alpine A610, (pronounced *alpeen ay-six-ten*) and it remained my top two-door coupé until its demise about four years later. It had a couple of small seats in the back, making it a 2+2 but its plastic body did little to deter people from thinking it was very much a poor man's Porsche. But there were at least a few of us who appreciated how good it was and it still gives me a lot of pleasure when I see the odd one passing by – once a year, if I'm lucky.

Produced in France by the motorsport-derived Alpine car builder, it was powered by a 3.0-litre V6 engine that dished out 250bhp without fuss or much lag from the turbocharger. Hit the throttle and the power's almost instantly there for you. The chassis was so well-engineered that you could throw it through the bends with the reassurance of the best-handling hot hatch and its enormous amount of grip would give you the confidence to go even faster. If you ended up giving it a bit too much welly too soon on the exit of a slippery corner, the back end would slide but predictably so.

The five-speed manual gearbox had a fantastic feel to each throw and the brakes were equally up to the job of controlling this 165mph machine. It was reasonably refined to drive on long journeys so it made a pretty decent grand tourer but it wasn't the most practical model, despite being wider and longer than a 911. The Alpine's nose was already home to a fuel tank and spare wheel so bags were best chucked on the back seats or left at home if you had passengers.

I think it would still fare well against today's competition in a cross-country dash but I doubt its interior will – it already played second fiddle to the chassis department when new. I'll always have a soft spot for it, though.

THE FACTS

Engine: 3.0-litre V6 turbocharged

Performance: 0–60mph in 5.4 seconds, 165mph

Price: £37,980

74. MERCEDES-BENZ SLS AMG

In the autumn of 2009, the monster German manufacturer unveiled its SLS AMG supercar, set to become the main rival for McLaren's MP4-12C. These two companies at one time joined forces to produce the Mercedes-Benz SLR McLaren but have since gone their separate ways. That is good news for us, because it breeds competition and gives us two cars to lust after instead of one.

"A rear spoiler pops up to see action above 75mph."

The most striking feature about the SLS has to be its gullwing doors, which are hinged on the roof and hark back to the 300SL from the 1950s. They open up on gas struts but need to be pulled down by hand (manual labour, darlings) because an automatic closing system would have added unnecessary weight.

The rest of the design isn't quite so dramatic or as elegant despite the long bonnet, wide front grille and side vents doing their best to ape the classy details of the original. A rear spoiler pops up to see action above 75mph. Inside the car it's a little more business-like than beautiful, even though the sculpted seats are tailored with perfectly stitched leather and the metallic centre console makes a bold feature. Carbon trim sits on the options list.

Getting into it and across the wide sill requires some side-saddle moves. Once in place, the driver can alter the car's new seven-speed double-clutch gearbox and electronic traction control system to suit the mood, but an electronic control limits its 197mph top speed. It'll hit 62mph time in a totally unrestricted 3.8 seconds though, thanks to its V8 with 563bhp. That's less than the SLR McLaren, but this one has more torque. It's also got a launch control system for those who like to make a noisy scene leaving a venue and it's fitted with motorsport-derived carbon ceramic brakes to make it stop just as dramatically.

The SLS AMG has been used as the safety car for the 2010 Formula One season and its wonderfully deep voice has often come through my TV speakers as it leads the F1 pack, when needed. Even though its seriously seasoned racing driver, Bernd Maylander, pushes it to the limit most of the time, the F1 cars behind it barely maintain their optimum operating temperatures. That is the phenomenal performance of these racing cars compared to a road car.

The future looks a busy one for the SLS with a host of variants expected, including a roadster with a soft-top – so those gullwing doors will have to go – and there's also talk of an electric SLS. Well, if Tesla can make a two-seater car capable of hitting 60mph in under 4.0 seconds then this is clearly a viable option. There will also be a Series Black version to satisfy the most power-hungry drivers and a racing version to compete in the FIA GT Championship.

LEFT: It just looks fast, even static with its door open. Best avoid low ceilings when you next drive one.

THE FACTS

Engine: 6.2-litre V8

Performance: 0–62mph in 3.8 seconds, 197mph limited

Price: £155,000

73. HOLDEN HSV

I find it difficult not to fall for the charms of all things Australian. The Aussies have an appealing no-nonsense approach to life that's mirrored in the cars they make, most notably the vehicles from the Holden manufacturer and its HSV performance department. Holden Special Vehicles (HSV) is a special section that has the sole job of making certain Holdens go faster and look better. Its slogan, "I just want one", fits their products perfectly.

"The engines are so vigorous ... you'll get an instant facelift the moment you try and match the manufacturer's 0–60mph time of just over five seconds."

Holdens are incredibly popular in Australia, on and off the race track. Every year at the country's most famous Bathurst 1,000km race, there is a ferocious rivalry between a grid-full of V8-powered Holden Commodores and Ford Falcons. The passionate crowds are as vociferous as the cars and there's not a lot of love lost between fans and drivers alike.

The cars are as straightforward as they come too, with HSV taking a standard Holden four-seater saloon or pick-up truck and giving it some extra grunt. Some have been exported from Australia to the UK. They've been really well received by those of us who want the punch and noise of TVR but the practicality of a Vauxhall Insignia. There is a strong link between HSR and Vauxhall because the VXR8 super-saloon that's on sale in the UK is the same car that's in Aussie showrooms, albeit with a different badge and sprinkled with some HSV trimmings.

The first Holden HSV I drove was for *Top Gear* back in 2000 and I had the time of my life being a hooligan on an airfield, burning rubber faster than a tank of petrol. HSV was only a decade old at that time and had been set up as a joint venture between the Aussie-based Holden manufacturer and British-based racing driver Tom Walkinshaw, who went on to set up his own TWR racing team and eventually buy the Arrows F1 team.

There's very little sophistication or cutting-edge technology about the HSV cars, but what they do have is a bottomless bucket of grunt and noise. It's all brawn and very little brain and the GTS 6.0-litre car I tested was everything I expected it to be – big and full of muscles. Brilliant. And at one point its 412bhp made it the most powerful car on sale in Australia.

The engines are so vigorous and have so much torque that you'll get an instant facelift the moment you try and match the manufacturer's 0–60mph time of just over five seconds. A ferocious bit of kit wrapped in a saloon body big enough to catapult a family across the country, it definitely lacks the refinement of BMW's M5 super saloon, but the Holden HSV is a winner in my book.

LEFT: If this Holden was a man, I would beat down its door for a date. Grrrrrrr.

THE FACTS

Engine: 6.0-litre V8

Performance: 0–62mph in 5.2 seconds, 150mph+

Price: £N/A

72. JAGUAR XJ220

If you took a bar of soap and used it for a week, the shape you'd be left with wouldn't be too dissimilar to the XJ220. Streamlined to the extreme, Jaguar's super-expensive supercar was at one time the world's fastest production car with a titillating top speed of 220mph.

Its engine was only a 3.5-litre V6 but its twin turbochargers boosted power to over 500bhp and that was clearly enough. It could greet 60mph in 3.6 seconds without the need to change into second gear, 100mph arrived in around eight seconds and its acceleration on the way there was brutal, thanks to its race-based power plant. However, this was also a reasonably docile motor if you wanted to enjoy its stratospheric posing ability rather than its performance.

It was built by Jaguar's motorsport department so it came with all the toys you'd expect, including a race-derived suspension set-up, which was heralded as giving the Jag world-class handling with world-leading steering. Built in Britain in the early 1990s, it is the flattest car I've ever seen. It measured five metres long, half that in height and around two metres wide, but it had no excess flab whatsoever and was actually lighter than Lamborghini's Diablo and Bugatti's EB110.

The first time I saw one in the flesh was when I worked for *Top Gear*. We were hosting a live car show in a purpose-built arena at Silverstone, which we called "Top Gear Live" (the title obviously took some thought). Jeremy Clarkson was definitely the show's tallest presenter but he managed to curl his frame – and his large bouffant – into it with even a bit of room to spare.

The interior didn't feature any of the exotically designed dials or sumptuously finished switches that you'd find in abundance in Italian supercars. That's a shame considering its staggering price of £403,000. For that sort of money, I'd want the car's interior designer on 24-hour call to make me bespoke buttons when the mood took me.

LEFT: Undoubtedly the world's most famous promotional girl unveils Jag's super duper supercar. I know Princess Diana is quite tall, but note how short the 220 is.

It was all hand-built, though and just a limited number were made. Jag had hoped to produce 350 but the price and the market dictated that less than 300 actually emerged. Then, in 1994, the mighty McLaren F1 burst onto the scene with its even-higher top speed and more desirable credentials. But there was no mistaking the magic of the XJ220. It can still sit in a car park and stun a crowd into silence with its beauty, and it can also captivate its driver by catapulting them across land at very naughty speeds.

"Built in Britain in the early 1990s, it is the flattest car I've ever seen."

THE FACTS

Engine: 3.5-litre V6

Performance: 0–60mph in 3.6 seconds, 213mph

Price: £403,000

71. MASERATI GRAN CABRIO

This is Maserati's first four-seater cabriolet. It's based on the Gran Turismo coupé, but only shares a few body panels. The Pininfarina-designed beauty looks just as good with the multi-skinned roof up as down, a switch which can be done in 28 seconds. It costs just over £96,000 and is clearly aimed at the affluent because the options list includes pearlescent paint for a staggering £5,288 and an iPod connector for £254, which is more than the device costs.

Inside, everything is trimmed with perfectly stitched leather and in the back the two seats are sculpted individually and mirror the shape of the front ones. There's definitely room for four adults back there, though they sit very upright, which could become uncomfortable on long trips, and I'd recommend they all wear headscarves because the wind buffeting in the back is fierce. It's almost unnoticeable in the front, though, especially when you erect the wind stop (£588 option) behind the front seats to reduce turbulence by 50 per cent.

You'll want the roof down all the time once you've heard the intoxicating and addictive scream from the 4.7-litre V8 engine that Ferrari built to Maserati's specification. It dishes out 434bhp to the rear wheels via a six-speed automatic gearbox with steering-mounted paddles, as well as a lever down on the transmission tunnel, should you prefer.

I picked one up in Paris and drove it 600 miles south to Monaco for a *Fifth Gear* road trip, and it was one of the most rewarding film days I've had. In Paris, the car was the main attraction as its sharp looks and massive 20-inch alloy wheels stood out from the Renault and Peugeot superminis littering the streets. I drove round the oblong-shaped roundabout at the Place de la Concorde tourist attraction, flicked off the traction control and gave it a boot of oversteer, which set my day up perfectly. Very naughty, but very nice.

For the next six hours it was straight-line stuff along the motorway, stopping frequently for fuel as the Gran Cabrio was doing 20mpg. Although that figure doesn't seem too good, I wasn't hanging about. The car proved a proper grand tourer, eating up the miles in a relaxed and incredibly comfortable manner, so I still felt Paris-fresh as we neared Monaco at the end of the day.

"As I entered the famous tunnel, I pressed the 'sport' button to make the exhaust even louder…"

A few miles outside the principality we found a mountain road with razor-sharp hairpins to test the handling. I thought it the best yet in Maserati's range, but I felt it needed even sharper steering, more bottom-end grunt to get out of the corners quicker and beefier brakes to halt its near two-tonne weight coming back down the hills.

But these niggles were blown to dust as I drove it round the Monaco Formula One race track for a couple of laps. I felt like the luckiest girl in the world because it was the Sunday before the big race weekend and so all the red-and-white kerbing, metal barriers, painted grid positions, colourful banners and the biggest yachts were out in force. As I entered the famous tunnel, I pressed the "sport" button to make the exhaust even louder and powered through to drown my excited screams.

LEFT: Beaming with delight here because I'd just blasted my way through Monaco's F1 tunnel, squealing with pleasure in the process.

THE FACTS

Engine: 4.7-litre V8

Performance: 0–62mph in 5.3 seconds, 176mph

Price: £96,175

70. RENAULT CLIO

69. MEGANE RENA

68. VOLKSW

67. PEU

66

LTSPORT 250

GEN GOLF GTI

EOT 205 GTI

BMW X5

65. BMW Z3 M COUPÉ

64. BMW Z4

63. NISSAN SKYLINE GT-R

62. TVR

61. NOBLE M400

70. RENAULT CLIO
69. MEGANE RENAULTSPORT 250

If you can remember the Renault Clio TV advertising campaign involving Nicole and her Papa, then you'll surely recall the Clio Williams as one of the most iconic hot hatches ever. The two were around in the first half of the 1990s, and Renault launched the blue car with gold wheels as a celebration of Nigel Mansell's 1992 Formula One title in a Renault-powered Williams.

I t was a project of the French manufacturer's motorsport-oriented division and it made the perfect circuit car. It had a 2.0-litre engine with only 150bhp, but was a lot lighter than its modern equivalent so it was incredibly chuckable, fantastically rewarding and enormous fun for every driver; it appealed to all walks of life and all levels of talent.

I also loved the RenaultSport 172, and I ran one for a year in the early 2000s. With 172bhp it was light on its feet, had pin-sharp steering and a fruity exhaust note, which raised its volume at every exit. I enjoyed every single trip I did in that car, whether it was the two-hour motorway slog to Birmingham to do some voiceover work for *Fifth Gear*, or a fun run through the local lanes of Hertfordshire. It was always up for a good blast and incredibly eager to please. I wish I still had it.

Sitting at the top of the current Clio tree is the RenaultSport 200, which is bigger, more expensive and more powerful than ever. With almost 200bhp, its 2.0-litre engine loves to be up in the high revs and its ever-brilliant front-drive chassis has all the poise and grip to make this car great. All these sporty Clios deserve to be in my top 100 because they offer an incredibly high level of entertainment for a comparatively low price.

In the class above the Clio, Renault also has a winning car with its Megane RenaultSport 250 Cup. I think it's the best super-hatch of 2010, and it was the quickest round Rockingham race track when we put it up against a gang of arch rivals for *Fifth Gear*, which included Volkswagen's Scirocco R, Ford's Focus RS and the Mazda 3 MPS.

The Megane 250 Cup is the most hardcore version but at £22,500 it's £1,000 cheaper than the top model because it does away with leather seats, climate control and automatic headlights. That's no hardship though, particularly when you gain a limited slip differential, which splits the car's 251lb/ft of torque between the front wheels to stop the outside one spinning when accelerating through a corner; it has a stiffer set-up, too.

It also has something called a PerfoHub, which is a ridiculous name for anything, but it does a first-rate job of guaranteeing a stable front end when you accelerate as hard as you can. It also helps the car to hit 62mph in 6.1 seconds, which is marginally slower than the Ford Focus and VW Scirocco, but it's round the corners where the Megane RenaultSport Cup pulls out its magic. It needs to be driven really hard, though to get the best from the 2.0-litre turbocharged engine and the grippy tyres. Such an aggressive style doesn't suit the majority of the UK's roads, so if you do find yourself behind the wheel of one, then do yourself and the car a favour and book in for some track-day action. You won't regret it.

ABOVE: I try to quell my pre-race butterflies ahead of a six-hour race at Silverstone in 2009. My two team-mates and I went on to finish second in class. Result.

THE FACTS

Engine: 2.0-litre four-cylinder (Clio), 2.0-litre four-cylinder (Megane)

Performance: 0–62mph in 6.9 seconds, 141mph (Clio), 0–62mph in 6.1 seconds, 156mph (Megane)

Price: £16,710 (Clio), £23,160 (Megane)

68. VOLKSWAGEN GOLF GTI
67. PEUGEOT 205 GTI

I wish so much that both these cars were still made today with all their mid-1980s trimmings. At that time they represented the ultimate in hot hatch design, handling and performance, and they really can lay claim to being the grand-daddies of the hot hatchbacks we see today.

My favourite, though, is the Volkswagen Golf GTI, particularly the Mk II (mark two), which I loved so much that I bought one and still drive it enthusiastically despite 170,000 miles on the clock. It's a 1989 G-plate and it cost me £3,000 when I became its sixth owner in 1998. The original Mk I was also an utterly wonderful creation, but by the time I could afford to buy into the badge there weren't many decent examples left.

Under the bonnet of my 16-valve GTI is a 1.8-litre engine that loves to rev – my brother ran an eight-valve GTI for a couple of years as well and we soon established his had more bottom-end grunt to it. The five-speed manual gearbox is still a joy to slip through the gate despite the high miles, and I love the detail of a golf-ball that makes up the top of the gear lever – a touch of humour shown by the German manufacturer there.

The front-wheel-drive chassis turns in sharply and it reassures you throughout a bend, even if you've gone in carrying a tad too much speed, but it's best not to carry too much because there's no ABS to help you stop, nor airbags if you run into serious trouble. It's a real joy drive on country roads and I feel so excited every time I take my Golf out on a B-road blast. Compared to the rakish designs of modern hatchbacks like the Renault Megane and Honda Civic, the Golf's large glass area makes visibility a cherished asset.

My former racing-driver father owned the Golf's arch rival for a short while, a Peugeot 205 GTi 1.9, and we all loved its agility and cheeky looks. It weighed a paltry 880kg, which made it light and quick through the corners, but also a bit on the flighty side compared to the more surefooted Golf. There were two models in the GTi range – the lesser-powered 1.6-litre and the range-topping 1.9-litre 130bhp. This was best identified by larger holes (and fewer of them) in the alloys wheels and a "1.9" badge (as opposed to the "1.6" badge) above the petrol cap. There was an unmistakable rasp from the exhaust as you accelerated through the gears and the five-speed box was characteristically Peugeot in that it was notchy.

My favourite memory of Dad's 1.9 GTi was when he drove it like he stole it, having picked up an Indian takeaway to bring home. It was winter and the twisty roads had collected a lot of snow. Undeterred, Super-Dad powered on, only for the car to slide into a back- and half-roll into a soft white bank. The phrase "curry in a hurry" has never seemed so well-illustrated.

ABOVE AND LEFT: Just one look at these two classics makes me nostalgic, and I'm happy to help keep one more Golf on the road whilst I cherish every mile in my Mk II.

THE FACTS

Engine: 1.8-litre four-cylinder (Golf)
1.6-litre and 1.9-litre four-cylinder (205)

Performance: 0–60mph in 7.9 seconds, 130mph (Golf)
0–60mph from 7.6 seconds, 123mph,
to 8.6 seconds,120mph

Price: £6,245 in 1984 (205)
£10,894 (Golf GTi 16v)

66. BMW X5

Once upon a time, if you wanted to buy an off-roader your only choice was one of the Land Rover family. Then, in 1999, along came a 4x4 from the Bavarian motor company BMW which, until then, had kept its blue-and-white badge firmly stuck on saloons, coupés and sports cars. The X5 was a massive hit with upscale mummies and daddies, who bought into the image of its off-road capabilities, rugged looks and high driving position.

ABOVE: The X5 opened up the 4x4 market to the townies. It's also a treat for drivers who appreciate a great chassis as it will embarrass many saloon cars on a racing circuit.

I am a farmer's daughter, so I've grown up with tractors and Range Rovers, and seen these proper working vehicles put their 4x4 systems to the test every day. Although I knew the X5's mud-plugging technology would barely get used by most people, I fancied it from the off. There are plenty of people who think they take up too much space and too much petrol, but they are more efficient and greener than many a knackered old and inadequately-serviced Vauxhall Vectra still on the road. A self-titled SAV (Sports Activity Vehicle), the X5 is marketed as the car to transport you and your family to a multitude of outdoor activities – and it's got the ability to join in as well. But for me, the car's forte is on a racing circuit rather than anchoring a tug-of-war team.

It defies physics in the way that it hurls its 2,000kg+ weight around the tightest of bends, big tyres screeching in delight, and the massive brakes get ever-hotter as they scrub speed, when required. During a *Fifth Gear* shoot at Anglesey race circuit, at the north-westerly tip of Wales, the 4.8-litre V8-powered SE model I drove was more like a sports car than an off-roader. For a car that's 5ft 7inches tall (my dream height), there's not a huge amount of body roll, thanks to the superb suspension control. There's so little slack in the steering that it's like being at the wheel of the best hot hatch.

Inside, it's engineered and finished to the same high standards that BMW gives its more executive-oriented cars and has proved such a winner that more than a million have been sold worldwide to date. It's currently in its second generation and prices range from £44,000 to £58,000, with diesel, petrol and twin turbocharged V8s engines that boast CO_2 emissions from as low as 195g/km – a 2.5-litre turbo Ford Mondeo emits more.

As well as the four-wheel-drive system, there's an eight-speed automatic gearbox and leather seats as standard. Options include side-view cameras and a Lane Departure Warning system. It's a long way from Dad's tractors!

THE FACTS

Engine: 3.0-litre six-cylinder to 4.4-litre V8

Performance: 0–60 mph in 7.6 seconds to 4.7 seconds, 130mph to 55mph

Price: £43,980 to £78,860

65. BMW Z3 M COUPÉ

64. BMW Z4

For reasons that I consider a bit unfair, this car was nicknamed "The Ugly Duckling" by the motoring press. I admit that it's not the most aerodynamic of cars to come from BMW, but to call it ugly is rather harsh. It's also sometimes known as "the Baker's Van" and although it has a slightly similar profile to a bread van, the car is too low to the ground for it to be able to shift many loaves. However, I do know that it will shift a fair few crates of lager, because I rammed the back of one full-to-bursting on the return trip from watching the Le Mans 24-hour race in 1999.

ABOVE: BMW knows how to make a great handling car and both these sportscars are some of the company's finest. And practical - the Z3 M Coupé will hold a lot of booze.

Even with that load, the car still felt quick and agile enough to compete in the race itself – thanks to a 3.2-litre six-cylinder engine with 286bhp, and one of the finest chassis on the market. With that German reliability, 24 hours of hard driving would be more like a stroll up the high street for it.

BMW's acclaimed Z3 roadster hid underneath its controversial looks. The Coupé was only available in the top M (Motorsport) guise in the UK, though the rest of Europe had the choice of lesser-powered versions as well. The Z3 Coupé retained the roadster's two-door set-up. It was a great driver's car that responded instantly to what you wanted it to do, and it had plenty of poke for its light-ish weight. Consequently, it was able to stay with more powerful machines on any type of road.

It was huge fun – so much so that I almost bought a second-hand one not that long ago. Though just as playful as I remember, its age meant that I would have had to treat it with more respect than my heavy right foot would want. So, as a service to the M Coupé preservation society, and to my driving licence, I walked sadly away from the deal.

In 2002, in the US, and 2003 in the rest of the world, BMW launched the Z4, the car that superseded all Z3s. In 2006, the Z4 Coupé was on sale in M guise with a 3.2-litre straight-six engine. It was also available with smaller, insurance-friendly engines, but without the M trickery. The hot M version, though, had performance figures to out-gun a lot of other cars. Hitting 60mph took 4.8 seconds and its sleek, sharp design made it just as striking to look at. And like its predecessor, it was a total delight to drive.

"a total delight to drive."

THE FACTS

Engine: 3.2 -litre six-cylinder (Z3),
3.2-litre six-cylinder (Z4)

Performance: 0–60 mph in 5.3 seconds,
155mph (Z3);
0–60 mph in 5.0 seconds,
155mph (Z4)

Price: £40,545 (Z3), £40,000 (Z4)

63. NISSAN SKYLINE GT-R

It takes some restraint for me not to say Nissan Skyline GT-RRRRRRRR whenever I speak of this car, because it's a fabulous growler. No dainty flower this one, it's a beast of a machine. It wants to be driven as hard as you dare, with its four-wheel-steering and part-time four-wheel-drive systems ready to take some punishment.

"... you can't actually feel the wheels turn, you just notice how accurate the steering is."

In 1997 the car came to the UK with full Nissan warranty backing and became a big hit with the few people lucky enough to drive one, let alone own one. Badged the R33, only around 100 were planned for British shores, but I made sure I had my sticky hands all over one of them as I tested it for *Top Gear* magazine. I first clapped eyes on it at Snetterton racing circuit in Norfolk and thought myself one of the luckiest little ladies on the planet as I had the whole morning to thrash round all seven corners of the 1.9-mile flat track as many times as I fancied. Woohoo!

Under the bonnet was a 2.6-litre six-cylinder engine with a turbocharger that produced 277bhp. That may not sound all that juicy, but it was more than enough to see the car rocket from a standstill to 60mph in 5.0 seconds. This put it smack-bang into the supercar territory of Honda's NSX and the Skyline was practical enough to carry four adults. Roaring down the main straight at Snetterton with the big exhaust booming in its wake, the car felt rapid. The power is fed to the rear wheels until they detect a loss of traction through the corners or in wet conditions, when it then gets distributed to all four corners.

The four-wheel-steering set-up is constantly active and working hard on every bend, as the rear tyres point away from the direction of the front ones to give as crisp and acute a turn-in as possible. Once the car has sensed everything has responded accordingly, the rear tyres turn back to follow the fronts for greater accuracy through the middle of the corner. Clever stuff, and it's so subtle that you can't actually feel the wheels turn, you just notice how accurate the steering is.

The car is a big one (15 feet long and over six feet wide), but it had the ability to shrink-wrap itself around me to become one of the most agile and engaging cars I've driven round a circuit. The cornering grip was phenomenal and encouraged me to get my foot down as fast and as hard as I could once we were at each corner's apex. I just had to remember to hang onto the steering and feed the gears in as quickly as possible.

It was breath-takingly huge fun and I managed to record my best (some might say worst) fuel economy figure ever at 6.3mpg. A great day's work. The latest GT-R has dropped the Skyline name and has much more power, with 478bhp from its 3.8-litre turbocharged V6. It's not quite so big as my Snetterton car, but it's just as fast and furious.

ABOVE: It's not one of the most glamorous cars in this book, but it has the performance to punch a hole right through it. Grrrrreat.

THE FACTS

Engine: 3.8-litre V6 turbocharged

Performance: 0–62mph in 3.5 seconds, 195mph

Price: £59,400 (latest)

62. TVR

TVR was a great British company that made sumptuously-sounding sexy sports cars. But the origin of its name is as far removed from its glamorous end products as possible: it was named after a man called Trevor! Trevor Wilkinson, in fact, who co-founded the company in the 1940s. It went on to become one of the country's biggest and best-loved car manufacturers ever.

"What a great legacy for a man with an unfashionable name."

The first time I took a real interest in TVRs was when the Griffith came out in the early 1990s. A 4.3-litre V8-powered muscle machine that could hit 60mph in 3.9 seconds and romp on to 161mph, and all for under £30,000. Oh yes, and it sounded like the earth splitting in two. It was quicker than a Porsche Turbo and needed a strong hand to keep it under control on fast, bumpy country roads.

At the same time the Blackpool-based company was well on its way to establishing a strong racing heritage with its long-running TVR Tuscan Challenge series, in which the then company boss Peter Wheeler regularly competed. Many GT racers cut their teeth wrestling these beasts around British circuits and they were really popular with drivers and race fans alike.

Along with the Griffith there were other equally well-named cars such as the Chimaera (pronounced *kai-mee-ra*), Cerbera (ser-ber-a), Tamora and Sagaris. I also drove a TVR, which sadly didn't have an evocative name, just a number – T350 – and my test became a popular YouTube hit – more due to the cold weather and thin top I foolishly chose to wear that day than the car's fabulous talents, which far out-weighed my own. In the second half of the 2000s there was another change of ownership and under new Russian rule I tested a Tuscan 2 for *Fifth Gear* with my fellow racer and co-presenter Jason Plato at the helm of a new Sagaris.

We both lit up their rear tyres and had their curvy bottoms swinging the full width of Anglesey's racing circuit. Jason drove the more stiffly set-up Sagaris on the limit with style and grace, and he was impressed with the car's direct steering and its 4.0-litre six-cylinder engine, which sent just over 400bhp to the rear wheels.

LEFT: If I adopted TVR's naming ceremony and created my own brand of motor-car, mine would be called VCK. Not good.

My Tuscan 2 was also a 4.0-litre six-cylinder but with only 350bhp, though it kept close to the Sagaris' tail throughout the day. TVRs are not really ideally suited to being everyday cars and the sheer muscle power I needed to change gear underlined that. The clutch travel reaches almost down to the car's headlights and it's a physical job to drive it quickly and sideways. These cars are best kept for sunny Sundays when you can submerge yourself in their wondrous power, thunderous noise and eccentricities – the exterior door-release buttons are under the door mirrors and they never fail to surprise and delight newcomers.

I always think of TVRs though as being a highly-powerful driving seat strapped to a rear-drive chassis, and wrapped in a stunning design that'll cost you somewhere in the region of £50,000. What a great legacy for a man with an unfashionable name.

THE FACTS

Engine: Usually big-litre V8s or six-cylinders

Performance: 0–60mph in around 4.0 seconds, 160mph+

Price: £50,000 or thereabouts

61. NOBLE M400

The car company Noble is a small, British-based two-seater sports car manufacturer that has now been in existence for more than a decade and is the darling of the petrol head world. It's a low-key, low-volume outfit that's made a big enough impact to take sales away from Ferrari with cars that have an enjoyable rear-wheel-drive chassis and juicy engines.

ABOVE: Noble has gone from zero to hero in the track day world with various models during its relatively short life so far. The future looks good for this UK firm.

"It could reach 185mph without missing a beat ... all for just under £56,000."

The first foray into the competitive market place was badged the M1,0 but this car was quickly replaced with the M12 in 2001 and it was so much better-looking that it would have been more at home on a race track. It performed like a race car too, with a 0–60mph time of 3.9 seconds and a top speed of 155mph from its 3.5-litre V6 with 310bhp.

Its acceleration is a bit brutal, but the chassis is a peach and makes every journey exciting and rewarding, especially if you do take it to a track day. It'll flatter most talents and its punchy engines will make you look really fast in a straight line at least. It was the circuit-focused version of the M12 that best suited my demands when I drove one at the Anglesey circuit in a twin test against a Mistubishi Evo VIII MR FQ 400. The Noble didn't have quite such a silly name – M400.

Based very much on the M12 but with a little more weight and a lot more power at 425bhp, the M400's superior power-to-weight ratio shaved almost half a second off the M12's 0–60mph time to become even quicker than a McLaren SLR. It could also reach 185mph without missing a beat, and all for just under £56,000.

Around the race track the M400 impressed me enormously with its endless energy and terrific torque all through the rev range. The steering was brilliant and kept me on top and in touch with the levels of grip underneath as this changed from corner to corner. It was precise too, no matter if I was pushing it through a quick set of bends or longer-flowing ones. The car didn't have anti-lock brakes, so I had to gauge the pressure perfectly to keep the wheels from locking up when I needed to scrub off the speed and in between

bends, the twin turbochargers threw us down the road.

The six-speed manual gearbox can be flicked through accurately and quickly but it can also behave in a much more relaxed fashion if you need a bit of a breather, or if you take off onto the main roads. And here the M400 turns from a full-on attacking machine to a docile companion that soaks up lumps and bumps with the refinement of a saloon car. Inside, it doesn't have the arresting beauty of a Ferrari, but fans of this car will be more interested to hear that it beat the grippier 4WD Mitsubishi Evo by almost two and half seconds a lap. How very noble indeed.

THE FACTS

Engine: 3.0-litre V6 turbocharged

Performance: 0–60mph in 3.5 seconds, 185mph

Price: £56,000

60. RADICAL SR3

59. ARIEL ATOM

58. MERCEDES

57. MAZI

56.

BENZ SL65 AMG BLACK SERIES

A MX-5

FORD GT40

55. FORD GT

54. FERRARI 456

53. BMW M1

52. LEXUS LF-A

51. MERCEDES-BENZ C63 AMG

60. RADICAL SR3

59. ARIEL ATOM

Track days have become increasingly popular over the last 10 years as they give everybody the chance to drive on some of the world's best motorsport circuits for a fraction of the price it costs to race. There are barely any limits to your choice of wheels – road legal or race-prepared, open-top or closed, diesel or petrol – but you must make sure all your tyre, water and oil pressures are spot-on and keep an eye on them throughout the day. Also, be aware that your brakes will take much more of a pounding than they do when driving on the road, so best let them cool down every so often.

ABOVE: As well as making a pair of striking looking cars, both these British companies have chosen fast-sounding names. Good work.

I took a BMW three-series diesel around Oulton Park a few years ago for *Fifth Gear* to highlight how accessible track days are, and it felt great to hassle some bigger-engined cars through the corners, even if they did leave me standing on the straights. If you need extra coaching there are usually some professional instructors on hand who'll share their racing secrets and help bring your lap times down, too.

There are a group of specialist manufacturers who make cars ideally suited for track days and I tested two of best against each other at Anglesey race track on a windy winter's day. A helmet, gloves and Arctic insulation are essential gear for both the Radical SR3 and Ariel Atom because there's not a door, roof, window or even a windscreen between them. They are both road-legal, though with registration plates stuck on wherever possible. Both cost around £28,000, hit 60mph in under 4.0 seconds and boast a power-to-weight ratio of a seriously compelling 400bhp-per-tonne. At the time, Radical boasted its SR3 was the fastest track day money could buy.

So I fired it up first, powered by a 1.3-litre engine Suzuki Hayabusa motorbike engine and if I wasn't firing on all cylinders before I slithered into it, I certainly was when I grabbed second gear off the line a few nanoseconds later. There is no room for comfort in the suspension set-up so it's great on a smooth tarmac circuit, but you do feel even the smallest bump through your whole body. There's precious little cushioning or sound-deadening anywhere, so the car's constant vibrations and high-revving engine screams are injected straight to your eardrums and soul.

It is phenomenally rapid so it's best to warm the tyres and brakes for a couple of laps before relying on them too heavily. Once hot, the car will turn sharply into a corner and you can't be too keen with the throttle because it'll oversteer sharply and test your quick reactions. This is not for the faint-hearted at all.

Its British-built Ariel rival was powered by a 2.0-litre Honda VTEC engine which was almost as happy to see its rev range nudge into double figures. It's slightly better suited to the road so its suspension is not so hard or as harsh, and when the rear end does break traction it slides out more progressively and is therefore easier to scoop up and pull back into line. It's not as frantic to drive as the Radical but just as exhilarating and you can drive it hard straight away.

But which was quickest? It was very close, but over a 1.2 mile-long lap the Radical was just 0.2 of a second faster with an impressive time of 53.3 seconds. Tiff Needell and I were mad enough to race a Radical at Brands Hatch for a two-hour, two-driver endurance race. We took the helm for a frenetic hour each and both dragged our carcasses out of the hot seat afterward to collapse in a steaming heap as we learned how to breathe again: they are relentless!

THE FACTS

Engine: 2.0-litre Honda VTEC (Ariel),
1.3-litre Suzuki Hayabusa (Radical)

Performance: 0–60mph in sub-4.0 seconds,
around 150mph (Ariel),
0–60mph in sub 4.0 seconds,
around 150mph (Radical)

Price: £28,000 (Ariel), £28,000 (Radical)

58. MERCEDES-BENZ SL65 AMG BLACK SERIES

The Mercedes-Benz SL500 has to be one of the most elegant cars ever built. I love the look of the 1960s original as much as the modern versions. It's a car that conjures romance, with its long, elegant bonnet and convertible hood, and each time I see one I think of driving off on a long journey with mischief in mind and a picnic in the boot.

"If this first effort is a benchmark then we can expect some exciting things."

But it's the most powerful AMG-wrapped SL65 Black super coupé that's my favourite. Just 350 will be sold, with only a handful of right-hand drive versions making it to the UK and the bulk heading for homes in the States AMG's core market. It's packed with F1-derived technology and we can expect more models to come in the future with the Black Series badge. If this first effort is a benchmark then we can expect some exciting things.

It is based on the SL65 AMG but has more power and 250kg less weight. The metal folding roof has gone in favour of a lighter aluminium and carbon-fibre fixed roof, and a retractable rear spoiler. That emerges only when you've bust the UK national speed limit of 70mph (hello, Officer), but it's an essential aid in assisting aerodynamics when travelling fast. Its extended wheel arches are as pumped as a body builder's biceps, and right at the front there are three large ducts and two bonnet vents to help keep everything cool under pressure. At six and a half feet wide, it gets noticed.

Under the bonnet is the fastest engine of the SL range, a hand-built 6.0-litre twin turbocharged V12, with a massive number of horses, enough to power an army – 663bhp. The SL's bonnet had to be redesigned to fit it in, and a sturdier five-speed automatic gearbox replaces the SL's seven-speed box. There's Mercedes-Benz's electronic wizardry which makes the throttle "blip" on every down-shift to match the incoming revs with the outgoing ones so it makes you look and sound like you're a brilliant pilot.

The phenomenal power is kept reasonably well reigned-in during slow town work, thanks to the way the engineers have made the V12 as user-friendly as possible at low revs. Once you're done with the city streets, it strains at the leash to eat the road in front and anything else in its path. It somehow manages to surge forward in a refreshingly velvety and calm fashion though, so it's not an intimidating beast for people who aren't used to such vigour.

It offers a ride that's on the firm side of firm and a soundtrack that'll have you reaching for the revs, even when you're stationary. The best place for this car is a circuit, and that's exactly where Mercedes-Benz expects its owners to be for the majority of their time with the Black Series.

ABOVE: Hit 75mph and the rear spoiler rises to aid downforce, but could attract unwanted attention in the process. So much for stealth.

THE FACTS

Engine: 6.0-litre V12 supercharged

Performance: 0–60mph in sub-four seconds, 220mph

Price: £214,000

57. MAZDA MX-5

If you're looking for the world's most affordable sports car and want it to also become one of the most fun cars you'll ever drive, then this is it. Mazda's MX-5 has changed little since its birth and is still one of my most frequently recommended cars when I'm asked for a two-seater convertible that won't break the bank. It offers so much for a car that's not even big enough to fill your garage. I'm always excited as I step into one because of the uncomplicated joy of it and I've tested various MX-5s on kart tracks, open air fields and busy public roads and always had a cheeky time in them.

"The five-speed manual gearbox had a short and snappy throw to it ..."

It cost just over £14,000 back in the early 1990s, and was fitted with a 1.6-litre 114bhp engine, which hit 60mph in 9.1 seconds and ran out of puff at 114mph. Admittedly that wouldn't set much on fire, but it had so much character it was a hoot, even when parked. A larger 1.8-litre was later fitted. It had, and still has, one of the simplest interiors you could wish for, with great ergonomics, well before that phrase ever became fashionable.

I was lucky enough to go to Hiroshima ,Japan, where the car was built, to attend the launchI. immediately fell for it, especially its door handle, where you put just one finger behind and pull gently. It was a wonderful attention to detail that I was deeply saddened to see replaced by bigger grab handles in subsequent models, because women complained they broke fingernails. Tragic.

Mazda had prepared a special twisty course against the clock to enable us competitive journalists to test the car's agility and performance. As soon as I was a quarter of the way through the two-minute course I knew the MX-5 was a winner. The steering and throttle response were so instant that I cracked a big grin and a giggle as the nimble car darted from one turn to the next with great precision and the athleticism of a cat.

The five-speed manual gearbox had a short and snappy throw to it, which made the car feel sporty and faster than it actually was. Plus the exhaust note had a fruity edge, which enhanced the illusion too. Today the cheapest MX-5 costs just under £17,000 for the entry-level 1.8-litre 124bhp engine. It is actually slower to 62mph than the original, taking 9.4 seconds, but is now fitted with more safety features such as anti-lock brakes and power steering, which add weight.

The most expensive £21,654 2.0-litre model has a 158bhp engine, which takes 7.9 seconds to reach 62mph and also comes with a hard-top roof to sit alongside the traditional soft-top. I tested both old and new 1.8-litre versions at Anglesey race track for *Fifth Gear* and I felt better connected to the older car, thanks to its really direct steering and little body roll compared to the newer car, but both were enormous fun.

The result? The younger car was a second per lap quicker but both cars underlined the fact that Mazda makes the best entry-level sports car for not a lot of money.

ABOVE: The door handles on the yellow MX-5 are a brilliant design, but every model makes the perfect 'my first sportscar'.

THE FACTS

Engine: From 1.8-litre four-cylinder to 2.0-litre four-cylinder

Performance: 0–62mph from 9.4 seconds, 122mph to 7.9 seconds, 131mph

Price: from £16,795 to £21,645

56. FORD GT40

55. FORD GT

If I didn't include Ford's GT40 in my top 100 my father would disown me. It's his ultimate dream car and if I had the cash, of course I'd buy him one – and thereby secure my place as his most favourite child in the process. Tee hee!

"Such is its attraction that even Jeremy Clarkson bought one."

This car was first and foremost a racer, with the road-going versions coming later. It was Ford's dream to build a car to compete in long-distance races and ultimately win Le Mans. That dream came true because the GT40 went on to win the gruelling 24-hour race at Le Mans no less than four times in the 1960s. My dad clearly has fabulous taste.

The car had the assets to make it a brilliant racer, as it was powerful and sat low to the ground. It was just 40 inches tall, hence the name, and was originally powered by a 4.2-litre 350bhp V8. Various other V8 engines were fitted during its lifetime.

With collaboration from the racing car manufacturer, Lola, the British-built prototype was launched at Heathrow on April 1, 1964. Perhaps not the most auspicious date they could have picked, April Fool's Day. They chose a lucky partnership with Gulf though, as its orange and pale blue colours adorned the cars that won Le Mans in 1968 and 1969.

The doors of a GT40 hinged in the middle of the roof, so as they open up they look like the wings of a landing eagle. Contrastingly, I've yet to see anyone enter or exit the car with equal grace because there's a really wide sill you have to clamber over to get into your seat – but it all adds to the fabulous drama of the car.

I think it has one of the most exotic shapes I've seen on any car – and Ford clearly thought it was a winner too. When the company made the car's spiritual successor, the GT in 2002, the scoops, bulges and profile of the original could clearly be seen.

The GT was launched to celebrate Ford's 100th birthday and to highlight the company's racing heritage. It was built in America and just over 4,000 were made. Only 101 were shipped to Europe, of which a mere 28 made their way to the UK. They are rare, but a friend of mine was savvy enough to get his hands on one. Naturally, it's his absolute pride and joy, which he wraps in a duvet every night.

Ford's blue oval badge may not have the same exoticism as Ferrari's prancing horse or Lamborghini's raging bull, but everything about the latest GT is spectacular. It's a car that demands your attention, makes your eyes pop out and your jaw fall slack, and that's before you've even opened a door. Such is the attraction that even Jeremy Clarkson bought one.

Then there's the thunder that erupts from the 5.4-litre supercharged V8 engine as it delivers 550bhp to those fat rear tyres. The performance figures are equally mouth watering, with a 0–62mph time of 4.0 seconds and a top speed of 205mph – although one was clocked at 211.89 at the Nardo test track in Italy. Paying homage to the original, a few heavily modified versions were turned into racing cars to compete in various championships around the world.

LEFT: Wow. Perhaps the best colour scheme on any car, ever. Its tarmac-hugging stance makes me want to run over and jump in, as does its successor (above).

THE FACTS

Engine: 5.4-litre V8 supercharged (GT),
4.2-litre V8 (GT40)

Performance: 0–60mph in 4.0 seconds,
205mph (GT), 0–60mph in not
many seconds, 200mph (GT40)

Price: £120,900 (GT),
£priceless (GT40)

54. FERRARI 456

This car was launched in 1992, when my love affair with Italian stallion motors started. At the time it was the world's fastest four-seater production car. It could hit 188mph, and reach 60mph in 5.2 seconds. Unusually for a Ferrari it had two rear-scooped seats complete with full-size seatbelts – that suggested enough room for adults, but leg room wasn't generous by any means.

"I grabbed the key, ran outside and spent the next few minutes stroking the car."

Its front-engined V12 with 436bhp made it the company's second most powerful of the time – the 478bhp F40 taking the top slot. More than 1,500 were built, with almost 150 coming to the UK. A further 400-odd were made a few years later with an automatic gearbox and given the badge GTA.

It was about a year after its launch when the six-speed manual GT became the first Ferrari car I ever drove. At the time I was working for *Carweek* magazine, EMAP Publishing's now-defunct weekly mag, and living out my dream job as a Road Tester. The office was just off Farringdon Road, not too far from Holborn in London, and parking right outside the office was at a premium. Ferrari's delivery driver had double-parked the 456 outside the office door and it needed to be moved as soon as possible. Well, someone had to do it.

I grabbed the key, ran outside and spent the next few minutes stroking the car: I fell in love with its Pininfarina-designed smooth body panels, perfect profile and well-proportioned rear end. I ran my fingers over every curve, opened the door, made the headlights pop up and down and then settled into the big seat and turned the key. Then I promptly sat and listened to the engine for a long, long time before shutting the door and guiding the thin, ball-topped gearlever into first and away.

I had no intention of driving the mere 500-metres round to the back of the building to a secure parking spot. Off I slipped through the streets to road test it in an urban setting – for as long

as I possibly could. The sounds of the V12 were glorious bouncing off the tall buildings lining some empty, narrow streets. It was totally addictive. I found myself revving the engine whenever traffic brought me to a standstill too, hopeful I was surrounded by fellow petrol heads who would appreciate the noise and childhood antics of my right foot.

Being at the wheel of the navy-blue 456 made me feel so special that I could fully appreciate why it cost the princely sum of £175,000. Eventually it was replaced in 2004 by the 612 Scaglietti, but never lost its spot in my affections.

ABOVE: Many years after my first dalliance with a 456, I filmed one for a buying guide on Fifth Gear. It was a car that didn't age particularly well, but I'd still have one in my dream garage.

THE FACTS

Engine: 5.5-litre V12

Performance: 0–60 mph in 5.2 seconds, 188mph +

Price: £145,999

53. BMW M1

BMW's most powerful strand is instantly recognized by the much-admired "M" badge. It stands for motorsport, but in my opinion, it should mean "mmm mmmm!" as it always guarantees delicious performance.

ABOVE: If only you could buy this for its original £30,000 price now. I'd take two. You can almost see the air part infront of it as its razor sharp nose cuts through. Lovely.

The motorsport strand has its own department within the German manufacturer and this M1 was the first car to emerge from it. It was created to race in the 1979 and 1980 ProCar series. This was a global championship that supported some of the Formula One races, and it had a reasonably high profile in the motorsport world. In fact, five F1 drivers, including Nelson Piquet and Niki Lauda, took part in various races. The idea was that these professional drivers competed against 15 privateers in a dash for cash. The winner received $5,000, and $50 was given to non-GP drivers for every lap of the race they led. Imagine if that could happen today – what a hoot.

At the drawing board stage for the M1, BMW called in the design guru Giugiaro and his ItalDesign team. They came up with a streamlined shape that fitted snugly over BMW's mid-engined rear-wheel-drive chassis. Giugiaro's creation instantly became a classic and an inspiration to many creators who followed. It had pop-up headlamps, a super slim grille, a hefty back end with slats over the rear screen and solid wheels. Together, they did a magical job of making it look retro and futuristic at the same time and I would definitely have one in my dream garage on its looks alone.

But it was also very performance-oriented, with a 3.5-litre straight-six engine that sat behind the two seats. This was the first and last time BMW built such a configuration, the rest of their models having engines in the front. It dished out 277bhp via a five-speed manual gearbox to hit 60mph in 5.6 seconds with a top speed of 162mph for the road car. The ProCar racing M1 had 470bhp, and there were even turbocharged versions with a staggering 850bhp – more than a modern F1 car – which raced in other championships.

BMW needed to build at least 400 road-going versions of the M1 to enable the racing cars to be homologated and therefore legal to compete, as per the rules. In the end, 456 cars were actually built, of which 49 were racers. But the German manufacturer also wanted the car to be as practical as possible and to make it viable for everyday use, so it was built to the company's world-renowned high standards with great reliability. Its road manners were equally top-notch, so it was just as comfortable on long trips as it was surefooted on shorter, twisty ones.

For those of us too young to fully appreciate the magnificence of the M1, BMW has kindly created a modern concept car, simply called the M1 Homage, which hints at what a future M1 could look like. Like the original, it boasts the double-M badge at the back and near-solid wheels. Come on, BMW, you know it makes sense!

"… I would definitely have one in my dream garage on its looks alone."

THE FACTS

Engine: 3.5-litre six-cylinder

Performance: 0–60 mph in 5.6 seconds, 162mph

Price: £30,000

52. LEXUS LF-A

Lexus is the upmarket arm of Toyota and is perhaps best known for offering the world one of the first large 4x4s to have petrol and electric power (a hybrid) in its RX model range. It also offers a luxury saloon, the LS, for £91,381. Until now that had been the Japanese company's most expensive model, but Lexus has just gone banzai and launched a very special motorsport-derived supercar with a price tag of £325,000.

"... before I stepped in, I was reminded that the car was pretty much priceless."

Called the LF-A (Lexus Flagship), it is pitched against the likes of Lamborghini's Murcielago and Aston Martin's DBS. It has been in development for a seriously long time. Lexus built it as a halo model to be unveiled when Toyota won its first Formula One race, but that never happened. It's been such a long wait for Lexus to make the decision to launch it anyway that the car's Formula-One derived V10 engine is no longer in racing use as they've all switched to V8s and Toyota is no longer in the sport.

A racing version of the LF-A took the main role of being the road car's test mule, and as such took part in the Nurburgring 24-hour race on two occasions. One of the drivers was the President of Toyota, Mr Akio Toyoda (odd, but correct spelling). The grandson of the company's original founder, he obviously has faith in his product. Apart from the costs associated with such a mammoth timescale, other reasons for the LF-A's seriously-high price are that only 500 will be made and that most of the car is made from aluminium.

The two-seater isn't as beautiful as many of its European rivals but it's certainly striking. It has an unmistakable Japanese look to it, with its sharp edges and angular vents. Inside, the details include elegant carbon-fibre indicator stalks and aluminium pedals. Underneath, it shares the same DNA as Lexus' more sedate and smallest saloon, the IS, but it's powered by something a lot more potent – a high-revving motor (up to 12,000rpm) with 552bhp. Its performance figures aren't so impressive as the cheaper Lambo Murcielago, though, with 62mph taking 3.7 seconds and a top speed of "only" 202mph.

I drove the racing-car version at Goodwood Motor Racing circuit in West Sussex on a very wet day and before I stepped in, was reminded that the car was pretty much priceless. No pressure. The race car's body was made from carbon fibre-reinforced polymer with a big rear spoiler and it stood just 48 inches from the ground – a Mazda MX-5 is taller. It also had just the driver's seat, was left-hand drive, and the centre console and dashboard crammed with buttons like a plane's cockpit.

After warming it – and myself – up for a lap, I began to push on and found the V10 engine sounded just like a F1 car from the early-2000s. The six-speed gearbox was a sequential design, with paddle-shifts that worked with the lightning speed that you need for racing. The steering was incredibly crisp and the suspension pretty much non-existent, but it made the car handle incredibly well and made me want to race it. Very much.

LEFT: Here's proof for those who believe putting more stickers on a car does make it go faster – 202mph enough for you?

THE FACTS

Engine: 5.0-litre V10

Performance: 0–60mph in 3.7 seconds, 202mph

Price: £325,000

51. MERCEDES-BENZ C63 AMG

In 2007 Mercedes-Benz fans welcomed the German company's new C63 AMG, a car that had the ammunition to convert devotees of BMW's M3. Very much the flagship of Merc's C-class range, it's bursting with goodies from the company's tuning arm AMG. The four-door saloon is the beefiest-looking in the range, with a deep-front spoiler, bonnet ripples, body bulges, big wheels and exhaust pipes. Its engine statistics are equally mouth watering, with its hand-built AMG 6.2-litre V8 producing 451bhp. This is statistically more impressive than BMW's smaller 4.0-litre V8 with 37bhp less.

ABOVE: If I'd been let loose with the crayon, I'd have added four more exhausts because this quartet look so good. If I owned one, I'd find it hard to keep it in a straight line.

The AMG rockets to 62mph in 4.5 seconds and on to a limited 155mph, but it does so in such an entertaining way that I couldn't wait to show off its talents to the real Rocket, snooker's Ronnie O'Sullivan, when he asked *Fifth Gear* for some help in choosing his next motor. The former three-times World Champion, Ronnie is known for playing his table game quickly, so we thought this C63 AMG would provide him with the pace he's familiar with. We went to a racing circuit, too – Castle Combe in Wiltshire, with its near-two-mile track, mild undulations and fast bends.

For the first part of the morning I showed Ronnie what the car could do, and knew it would appeal to the boy in him as much as it did the little girl in me, because the Merc lit up its rear tyres in clouds and clouds of smoke every time I went sideways. I loved it and Ronnie loved it too, asking how I did it. I returned the compliment by asking about his record-breaking 147 maximum which he'd achieved in a World Championship game not long before we met.

He told me that as soon as he hit the first ball he knew he'd clear the table, which I found astonishing, but then I released that there is a similarity to racing drivers who know they've hooked into a fast lap pretty early on, too. From the moment you start the engine the AMG is an entertaining car and it rumbles into life with its soft, but deep V8 tone. As it has almost as much torque as power, 442lb ft of it, there's bags of get-up-and-go to make it seriously shift into the future.

"I loved it and Ronnie loved it too, asking how I did it."

With the traction control off, an alert pair of hands to keep the seven-speed gearbox in the right cog and a keen right foot, the C63 danced to my tune unbelievably effortlessly. A great chassis and a brilliantly-matched gutsy engine made one-handed power slides look like child's play. It's a great car for showing off.

And then it was Ronnie's turn. He showed that he definitely has a natural feel for what the car's doing, and he was going so well I taught him how to do a doughnut – a quick trick, but incredibly rewarding. I was really pleased to see that about a year later he took part in his first motor race, though in a less-hairy Volkswagen Jetta. A great car and a great man. Did he go on to buy it? Well, he said he would.

THE FACTS

Engine: 6.2-litre V8

Performance: 0–60mph in 4.5 seconds, 155mph

Price: £52,435

50. PORSCHE CAYMAN

49. PORSCHE CAYE

48. LOTUS EV

47. ALFA

46.

NE

RA

ROMEO 8C

ALFA ROMEO 8C SPIDER

45. BENTLEY CONTINENTAL GT SPEED

44. HONDA S2000

43. FERRARI CALIFORNIA

42. BUGATTI EB 110

41. CATERHAM SEVEN

50. PORSCHE CAYMAN

49. PORSCHE CAYENNE

After Porsche announced details of the Cayenne, the company's first non-traditional sports car in the first half of the millennium, brand aficionados were ready to wash their hands and walk smartly away. When the company's first sports utility vehicle made its initial appearance the same people thought the designers had lost the plot and been too heavy-handed with the ugly stick.

RIGHT: Some may think this is a poor man's 911, but owners of the Cayman will have the last laugh. Here's an incredibly rare sighting of a Cayenne — off-road.

"Own one of these and you acquire membership to an exclusive club..."

Being a fan of the underdog in almost all situations, I immediately warmed to the Cayenne and once I'd driven it I was smitten – the old adage "try before you buy" never seemed more apt. I've driven many of them now on all roads, including a variety of racing circuits across the country, and it never fails to impress me with its sports car handling and high -performance engines ranging in power from 300bhp to 500bhp. All this from a fairly sizeable car that also has pretty competent off-road skills, too.

Perhaps the most telling test I did was in a Cayenne GTS, just one model under the top-spec Turbo, and pitted it against BMW's X5 SE. Both cars had 4.8-litre V8s engines and although the Porsche had 50bhp more power at 405bhp, it was also the heaviest.

But it didn't feel it as we barrelled round the Anglesey circuit at full pelt. It loved being thrown from left to right and there wasn't even a hint of body-roll as it switched direction, thanks largely to Porsche's brilliant active stability wizardry. The steering was smooth and accurate, so it was an easy job for me to place it on the racing line through each bend. Then there was the phenomenal grunt out of the corners, which made it a whole two seconds quicker than the BMW, a fact I would have found hard to believe at the beginning of the day. Consequently, the Cayenne GTS overtook the X5 as my number-one SUV. And with a peace-keeping hybrid petrol and electric version due soon, it could win even more fans.

Another of Porsche's cars to miss out on the good publicity it deserves is the Cayman. Overlooked and underrated by too many, it's still one of my firm favourites. It is based on the Boxster but has a coupé body style, with an aerodynamic roofline and prominent haunches. Inside, the quality is every bit as good as you'd find in a 911 and it's a car that draws just as much attention because there aren't that many of them about. Own one of these and you aquire membership to an exclusive club that really shouldn't be so secret. This is one of the motoring industry's cars that needs to be shouted about and I urge people to get out of their Mercedes-Benz SLK and into one of these. The Cayman is so amazing that the lack of folding roof will never be a concern, I promise.

Launched in the mid-2000s, it sits between the Boxster and the 911 in the company's model range and it won the Top Gear Sports Car of the Year and various other credible awards as soon as it went on sale. It's a fantastic car and gave me one of my most memorable road trips from London to Exmouth, two-up with a week's worth of luggage secure under a big net behind the seats and in the nose. It cruised brilliantly along the M3 and dual carriageways, then came alive on the undulating and demanding roads as we wound our way down to a small village. I didn't want the journey to end.

THE FACTS

Engine: From 3.6 V6 to 4.8-litre V8 (Cayenne)
From 2.9-litre to 3.4-litre flat-six (Cayman)

Performance: 0–60mph from 7.8 seconds, 143mph to 4.7 seconds, 173mph (Cayenne)
0–60mph from 5.7 seconds, 163mph to 5.1 seconds, 170mph (Cayman)

Price: From £41,404 to £81,589 (Cayenne)
From £37,261 to £45,449 (Cayman)

48. LOTUS EVORA

It had been a long time since Lotus gave us a brand new model, with the Elise more than a decade earlier. Inevitably, the motor industry was positively bursting with anticipation to get its hands and feet on the Evora in spring 2009. The near-£50,000 sports car may have been tailor-made for the original Elise generation, who had since grown up and sprouted a family, as the Evora is available as a four-seater, as well as with just two. The more passenger-friendly version is best described as a 2+2 to be honest, but I'm sure the kids can sit on their knees as they grow and allow Mum and Dad to cling onto their youth up front.

ABOVE RIGHT: It doesn't have the most mould-breaking design but this car still turns heads. The £200,000 Evora Cup GT4 racing car has 400bhp and was unveiled in 2010.

Despite this token of maturity, the mid-engined rear-drive Evora is still very much a car with thoroughbred handling. It's packed with enough Lotus know-how to take the rival fight to the door of Porsche's Cayman. The fact that it had a remarkably quick gestation – from drawing to road in just over two years – underlines the engineering genius within Lotus.

It has deep roots as a British company, having been the brainchild of Colin Chapman in the 1950s. The company went on to win many Formula One Constructors' titles as well as to make a variety of affordable sports cars for the road. It is currently owned by the Malaysian car manufacturer Proton, and turned to Japanese car maker Toyota to supply the engine here.

It's a 3.5-litre V6 from the humble Toyota Camry family car (not on sale in the UK), but it's been tweaked to make the Evora a 160mph sports car. It still retains the efficiency of a family saloon, with almost 33mpg. Its 276bhp isn't quite so powerful as the Cayman's 315bhp, but the Evora packs a lot into just a few revs. Its power delivery is so flexible you can make decent progress using only half the rev band. At this relaxed pace the car easily qualifies as a mile-munching grand tourer, plus it has the practicality of a boot big enough for a set of golf clubs.

But it's also incredibly energetic when you hit the throttle and make it dance round corners as its designers intended. Underneath, it's made in a similar way to the Elise, with a monocoque chassis and bonded aluminium, though it's more than two and half times stiffer than the smaller, older car. This helps give the Evora's steering its knife-edge precision. You feel every movement through that wheel and the slim Recaro seat, which forces you to sit low down in the car, where you're best-connected.

The suspension soaks up enough of the bumps to give a comfortable ride and it's good to see a driver-friendly,-six-speed manual gearbox. Only 2,000 will be made each year for the foreseeable future, which is small-fry compared to Porsche's output, but signals a big party for those hunting exclusivity.

THE FACTS

Engine: 3.5-litre V6

Performance: 0–62mph in 5.1 seconds, 162mph

Price: £49,875

47. ALFA ROMEO 8C

46. ALFA ROMEO 8C SPIDER

There are two words in the automotive world that cause grown men to become wistful and misty-eyed – Alfa Romeo. The marque conjures up fond memories of when they were young boys and when the Italian manufacturer made sporty cars like the Giulietta Spider, most famous thanks to its role as Dustin Hoffman's motor in the 1967 film, *The Graduate*.

ABOVE: Whilst the beautiful red head polishes her most sultry look for the world's paparazzi, the two motor show cleaners discuss how they can polish off their own vanishing trick.

"It really is a hairy-chested sports car, but it has the beauty of Angelina Jolie."

Not everyone shares this sentimentality, as some of us just aren't old enough for that, but everyone knows the older Alfas were much better suited to Italy's warmer climes than our rust-accelerating one. But most will agree there's definitely something about Alfa Romeo that tugs at the heart strings.

In 2009, when I drove Alfa's convertible version of its sexiest supercar to date, the 8C Spider, I almost wrote a cheque out before I'd turned the key. But even if I'd had £174,000 – £174 was more like it – that money wouldn't have bought me a thing because every one of the 500 made were sold before they'd even turned a wheel.

Nonetheless, I was determined to make the most of the rear-wheel-drive chassis at the car's launch at the company's test track in Balocco, northern Italy. In the metal, it's so beautiful that I lingered and lusted after its curves and bulges for much longer than I usually do – especially when there's a V8 engine waiting for my right foot.

This Spider is the younger sibling of the 8C Competizione coupé, which sold out within two weeks of being unveiled at the Paris Motor Show in 2006. In cabriolet form, its voluptuous rear end becomes even more gorgeous, especially when you drop the part-electric Z-fold roof. Its unique windscreen is made from carbon fibre, and there's much more of it throughout the cabin, alongside lashings of hand-finished aluminium, leather and a pair of seats as thin as a crisp, but bafflingly comfy.

The star is the engine, made with help from Alfa's stable-mates Ferrari and Maserati, and Ferrari liked it so much that a smaller version powers its California. If I could make a home for my ears right next to the Spider's four exhaust pipes, I would. It certainly has the "unmistakable voice" that the audio department insisted on in the development stages, no matter where the revs are in its 7,500rpm range, in any of the six gears.

And these were all thoroughly tested on the circuit's combination of straights and twists, where the car's rear 20-inch tyres will break traction once the 450bhp has been let loose and the traction control turned off. Eighty per cent of its torque is on tap from a lowly 2,000rpm and this helps it to shoot out of slow corners like a whippet out of the traps – even though it weighs 1,675kg, 90kg heavier than its coupé sister.

It really is a hairy-chested sports car, but it has the beauty of Angelina Jolie. Though she'd probably be more practical, because the near-useless boot space will force you to put a suitcase in the seat next to you, or a passenger. I know which one I'd choose.

THE FACTS

Engine: 4.7-litre V8

Performance: 0–60 mph in 4.1 seconds, 181mph (8C 4.2 seconds, 181mph)

Price: £174,000 Spider

45. BENTLEY CONTINENTAL GT SPEED

If you love the idea of owning a Bentley but don't fancy ever being a passenger in one, then the Continental GT is for you. This two-door grand touring coupé is the company's smallest, thinnest and shortest model, and it *almost* comes in with the thinnest price, starting at £126,500 (the entry-level Flying Spur is surprisingly a few grand less).

ABOVE: One of the most optimistically named cars as there aren't many places you can experience the Speed's top speed. Its shape and weight needs a lot of space to get there.

"... there is no place long and flat enough in the UK to reach 202mph ... "

If you love the idea of owning a car with a fast name, then the GT Speed is definitely for you – when it was launched in 2003, you were getting the keys to the cheapest 200mph showroom car money could buy.

I drove it for *Fifth Gear* at a motoring industry test facility in Bedfordshire called Millbrook. As well as having some challenging hill routes, off-road courses and rough surface sections, there's also a two-mile banked bowl for top-speed testing.

I wasn't going to attempt any 200mph-runs despite Bentley saying this car will see 202mph, but I'd wait for whatever the conditions and my bravery would permit that day, and settle for what came up on the Speedo. If we had been thinking of testing it to the max, we would at least had to have put in a prudent call to Bentley's tyre experts and had them in attendance. The load on the rubber, particularly the outer two tyres, would be immense on such a continuously-banked circular track at that speed. So, with nothing more than a once-over of the tread depth and a kick, off I went. Such high-tech safety precautions...

Maybe the GT Speed should have the number 6 somewhere in its name because its performance figures are littered with it – it has a 6.0-litre engine that produces 600bhp at 6,000rpm. It will hit 0–60 in under six seconds, though – 4.3 seconds, to be precise. It's also packing a couple of turbos on its W12 engine that combine to make the car as smooth around town at 30mph as it is tearing around test tracks. It's so versatile.

But back to my high-speed caper. After a couple of laps (four miles) to warm myself up, I was at 145mph with the revs at 5250rpm in fourth gear and the throttle wasn't even stroking the carpet, so I continued to push hard and grabbed fifth gear to see the Speedo climb to 155mph.

The metal Armco that would (hopefully) stop me careering off upward (and then downward) if anything went wrong was whizzing by to my right. The car had squashed itself into the track, with the forces the speed had generated on its heavy body and I could sense the heat building in the low-profile tyres. I kept the steering steady and looked as far into the distance as the track would allow, then increased the speed again. The revs rose to 6,000rpm and the Speedo to 160mph in fifth, which proved to be my limit for the day as I didn't fancy any more on that circuit. Bentley even says there is no place long and flat enough in the UK for the car to reach 202mph – and they also told me that 160mph was as fast as their drivers had taken it at Millbrook, too.

THE FACTS

Engine: 6.0-litre W12-cylinder

Performance: 0–60 mph in 4.3 seconds, 202mph

Price: £144,400 Speed

44. HONDA S2000

Honda's two-seater sports car was born as a 50ᵗʰ birthday present to itself. I've spent many thousands of miles in them over the years, however, so I feel as though it was more of a gift to me, actually. So, thank you, Honda. It was launched in 1999, and that's when I had my first adventure with it during a test I wrote for *Top Gear* magazine and it ended up being the cover story. The car was thrust into a marketplace where Porsche Boxster's and Mercedes-Benz' SLK had ruled the roost for a few years having established themselves as *the* sophisticated sports cars to be seen in.

The S2000 (pronounced *S two thousand*) wasn't as pretty as its rivals, but this was a real bonus in my book. Even though I'm a girl, I admit that the Boxster and SLK can look a bit too girly and that might have put off some Alpha males along the way, too. The Honda's chiselled features make it more handsome than beautiful and widen its appeal as a result. Its long snout, clean sides and pert rear end have hardly needed the surgeon's knife during its 10 years, and every owner I've ever spoken to has nothing but praise for the way it looks. It's also given them endless joy, and if that wasn't enough, its reliability record is stunning as it either topped surveys or loitered close to the top for most of its life.

As is customary for all great sports cars, the S2000 is rear-wheel-drive and its handling as sharp as its looks. The steering is one of the most direct on the market and its feedback so thorough that it makes you feel an integral part of the car. It has one of the shortest and sweetest six-speed gearboxes and it's 2.0-litre engine is a firecracker. It's one of Honda's renowned VTEC variable valve timing units so it has a Jekyll and Hyde quality to its performance – below 6,000rpm, it has a spring in its step but it won't blow your socks off. But as soon as the revs hit that figure, it turns into a nutter as the engine unleashes an ever-rising scream that won't stop until you hit the heady heights of 9,000rpm. That's wandering into motorbike-revving territory.

Its 237bhp enabled each cross-country journey to be full of fun. It could hit 62mph in 6.2 seconds and on to 150mph, and in all my miles with a S2000 I never saw that figure, Officer, but got the best hair blow of my life. The electric roof is so quick to come down that you can do it while waiting for the traffic lights to turn green – an incredibly useful feature considering the UK's unpredictable weather. A hard-top was also an option for those wanting extra protection. I am truly saddened this car is no longer available but I wait in anticipation for Honda's next rear-drive winner.

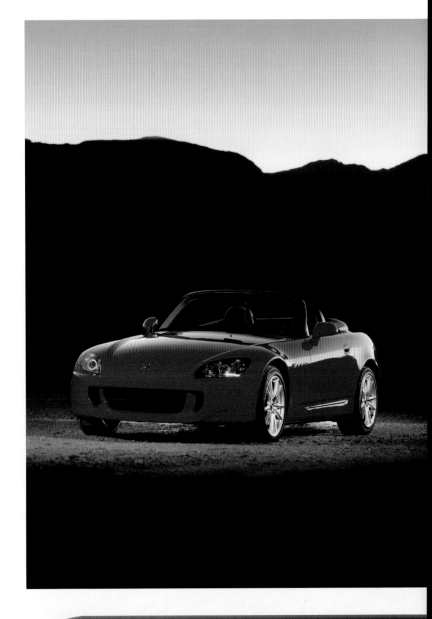

"… it's 2.0-litre engine is a firecracker."

ABOVE: Yes, this is me giving a lift to Damon Hill, Mario Andretti and Emmerson Fittipaldi. I just found them hitching on the M25.

THE FACTS

Engine: 2.0-litre four-cylinder VTEC

Performance: 0–60mph in 6.2 seconds, 150 mph

Price: £25,995

43. FERRARI CALIFORNIA

Ferrari California. In just 17 letters, the Italian dream maker joined two words to make a perfect marriage. The first brings exotic passion with a strong performance pedigree, while the second promises sunshine, smiles and stress-free days. A great match.

"So is the California a true sports car as well? Yes."

It has a great big price, too: £143,000 makes it more expensive than its two main rivals, the Bentley Continental GTC and the Mercedes-Benz Sl63 AMG. But it's got something in abundance that these two would love to have more of: sexiness. Its wide hips and bulbous bottom are the motoring equivalent of merging Beyoncé with Jennifer Lopez. Those lumps and bumps do nothing for its weight, though, as it's actually heavier than the V12-powered Ferrari 599.

Its curves become even more prominent when the California's electric-powered hard-metal roof folds down with a 14-second acrobatic display that marks a first for the marque. It's also the first time Ferrari has fitted a fuel-injected V8 engine under the bonnet and this front-mounted power plant is 4.3 litres in size and 453bhp in power.

It gets off the line to hit 60mph in a blistering 3.9 seconds, and romps on to 193mph, greedily chomping through the seven-speed twin-clutch gearbox – yet another Ferrari first. Its little steering-mounted paddles make changes quick and easy, whether you're on your way up the box or down it, and they are super smooth, too. Ease off the throttle for a bit, and the California shows it's just as capable of being a grand tourer as a sexy cabrio.

What better way to determine those racy credentials than with a test at Silverstone against an Aston Martin DBS Volante? That's exactly what happened when Jeremy Clarkson challenged me and the California to a duel as part of the shenanigans for his 2009 annual video, aptly called *Duel*. The Aston cost £175,681 and had a V12 engine with 510bhp, but it wasn't quite as quick to 60mph.

Even before we turned a wheel, the race was on to drop the tops in the quickest time and I managed to set off with a tiny lead. I'd set the Ferrari's controls to Sport mode with the traction control off so as not to hinder my performance, but the Aston was soon on my tail. There was a lot of pride at stake for both drivers and cars, and Jeremy and I

slid our way round each bend, swapping places for an energetic hour or two. The California's tail was so willing to slide that I needed some fresh rear rubber after about 20 minutes. Wicked!

There was plenty of comedy banter on the in-car walkie talkies too, whenever a straight bit of track gave us a moment to talk. And laugh – it was such a hoot that we carried on long after we should have stopped, forgetting the cameras and just relishing each lap in two fabulous cars. So, is the California a true sports car as well? Yes. It slides like one, and while it lacks the thoroughbred agility and crisp turn-in of the F430 supercar, for the laughs it gave me that day, I'd definitely call it a supercar.

LEFT: Most days I love my job, but when I go to the launch of a new Ferrari I *really* love my job.

THE FACTS

Engine: 4.3-litre V8

Performance: 0–60 mph in 3.9 seconds, 193mph

Price: £143,325

42. BUGATTI EB 110

The Bugatti EB 110 (pronounced *Eee Bee One Ten*) was once the darling of the brand, back in the early 1990s, before the Veyron stormed in to steal its thunder. It was made 110 years after the birth of Ettore Bugatti, the company's Italian founder, and only 139 were ever built – the accountants clearly over-ruling the sentimentalists, who probably thought 110 cars would be a good number to build. As it was, 139 still wasn't enough to make the company profitable and eventually it went on to be bought by the VW Group.

The EB 110 instantly took its place as one of the world's fastest cars, even being the bearer of the much sought-after title "fastest street-legal production car" for a while – demoting the Lamborghini Diablo, thanks to a top whack of 212mph. Its hand-built body was made from aluminium and its visual party piece were the doors that opened upward in a fabulously extravagant fashion. They gave the car a big wow factor whenever and wherever you arrived. A bit over-the-top perhaps when you're nipping out for some milk, but I think they're ace.

A glass window gave a great view down to the engine that sits just behind the two seats, and it's a sight worth seeing – this mid-mounted V12 has not one, not two, not three, but four turbochargers. It has a six-speed gearbox and a four-wheel-drive chassis to make the most of its 553bhp, and could send the EB 110 rocketing toward 62mph in 3.8 seconds – good enough to stick with the big boys today.

Despite being available only in left-hand drive, the EB 110 was praised for being user-friendly – think more sportscar than supercar – and its size helps, as it was smaller than Jaguar's XJ220 rival. This made the cabin a tight squeeze for anyone over six feet, tall though and this became the car's biggest fault because it restricted certain owners from making long journeys. It was a shame because the EB 110 boasted better-than-average fuel economy and a comfortable ride. However, my five feet five (and a half) inch frame would make me a perfect fit in its bucket seats, so every cloud has a silver lining for us shorties.

I've never had the chance of driving one, however, mostly because

ABOVE: Bugatti clearly had the blues when it came to painting its building and cars, but not when making high performance motors.

"Bit over the top perhaps when you're nipping out for some milk."

I wasn't mixing in the right company when it was launched – I was working as staff writer on *Max Power* magazine at the time, and more familiar with bass boxes in Beetles than with Bugattis. I've yet to drive the Veyron too, so I sadly sense a pattern developing here.

It was considered to be one of the more affordable cars for its class with the relatively small price of £285,500. That's a heck of a wedge of cash even today, but the Jag XJ220 at the time cost £403,000, which made the Bugatti look much more affordable.

THE FACTS

Engine: 3.5-litre V12-cylinder

Performance: 0–60 mph in 3.4 seconds, 212mph

Price: £285,500

41. CATERHAM SEVEN

The Caterham Seven is a car that comes in more guises than Rory Bremner. This may be one of the oldest designs on our roads for its barely-changed roots go back to the Lotus Seven of the 1950s. It is also one of the most adaptable cars and can be fitted with a variety of engines. At present there are 16 different variations with near-identical body shapes to chose from, starting with the 1.4-litre 16v 105bhp Classic up to the £42,000 Superlight R 500 SV with 263bhp. Caterhams may be small in size, but their numbers are anything but.

The Superlight will hit 60mph as quickly as a motorbike, taking just 2.8 seconds with a top speed of 150mph. That's plenty fast enough for an open-top two-seater with the aerodynamics of a brick. Caterhams are incredibly popular with people who love to build their own and I take my hat off to them for then having the courage to drive them – I wouldn't trust myself to drive something I'd built over 100mph!

I'm more than happy to race one, however, and to be among 30 identical Caterhams all jostling for the same piece of tarmac, heading into a bend at 100mph on a racing circuit. Some of the best fun I've ever had in motorsport was at the helm of a Caterham, in many various championships dedicated to the marque. One of the most memorable was at Snetterton in Norfolk, when I had a one-off race in a K-series-powered car for a *Top Gear* item. After half an hour of terrific battling, I crossed the finishing line a very happy sixth with a whacking great smile.

I also remember another race at Thruxton, though this time my younger brother Charlie was racing in the R400 Superlight series. The cars had about 200bhp and were on slick tyres (no grooves). And after clipping a kerb at the chicane in an overtaking move, his car fired itself into the tyre wall and he broke a vertebra in his neck. Thankfully he's fine now and although he's successfully raced since, he's not driven another Seven.

The latest Caterham I drove was during a test at the Anglesey race circuit for *Fifth Gear* in 2008. I drove a £43,000 CSR260 Superlight, powered by a 2.3-litre Cosworth engine, which was up against a Lotus Exige S. As well as being a couple of grand more expensive, the Superlight was 300kg lighter and almost a second quicker to 60mph than the Exige a Lamborghini-eating 3.1 seconds. On a wet track and with 260bhp in a car that weighed so little, its semi-slick tyres were spinning each time I put the power down in first, second and third gear, and the back end slid around at the tinniest invitation.

It was incredibly noisy and huge, huge fun, but after a couple of laps hitting 120mph, with plenty of sideways stuff round the corners, the roof started to pull away from the windscreen mounts and the doors wanted to fly off. It was a far cry from the coupé Exige, which even came with a cup holder. The Caterham came out the victor by two and a half seconds per lap, and I emerged happily ruffled.

LEFT: Caterham racing is incredibly popular and competitive for a variety of budgets. **TOP RIGHT**: Richard Dunwoody may be three times National Hunt Jockey Champion, but he's also a mean driver as I found out in our Caterham duel for a national newspaper.

THE FACTS

Engine: 2.3-litre four-cylinder

Performance: 0–60 mph in 3.1 seconds, 155mph

Price: £42,900 (CSR260)

40. BMW F1 CAR

39. BMW M5

38. ASTON M

37. ASTO

36.

RTIN ONE-77

N MARTIN VANQUISH S

MASERATI TROFEO

35. ASTON MARTIN DBS

34. ASTON MARTIN V8 VANTAGE

33. PORSCHE PANAMERA TURBO

32. PORSCHE BOXSTER

31. PAGANI ZONDA

40. BMW F1 CAR

39. BMW M5

The M5 is perhaps the most perfect family car because it's big enough and sedate enough for the kids, luxurious enough for the other half and downright powerful enough for the driver when the mood suits. It's also the only car I know to go head-to-head with a Formula One car. I know this because I was the jammy one who drove it.

ABOVE: If only this was street legal. For more space though, few cars can compete with BMW's four-door super saloon that behaves like a supercar.

"Traction control can be fully switched off too, which I duly did."

At the time, both cars were powered by the company's V10 engine, both had seven-speed gearboxes and both could do more than 200mph – but the M5 was the only one that could carry passengers. The F1-M5 race was an item for *Fifth Gear* in 2007. Much as I was incredibly fortunate to be one of the two drivers, it was Tiff Needell who really lucked out because he got to slide into the narrow cockpit of the F1 car.

We were at Rockingham race track in Northamptonshire, using its 1.9-mile track, which has 12 turns as well as a banked section. Of course we knew the F1 car was going to be quicker but we wanted to find out by just how much. It was the best twin test I've ever been involved in. Suited, booted and helmeted, I set off in the 507bhp M5. It has a default mechanism that initially sets the power at 400, but if that's not quite enough for you, a button unleashes the additional 107bhp. Traction control can be fully switched off too, which I duly did.

The Williams F1 team supplied the racing car. They didn't want to put it through unnecessary stress, so we weren't allowed to start the race from a standing position, as in a F1 race. We went for a rolling start instead. So we "crawled" round for half a lap at 70mph, on the approach to our flying start. I was in third gear, pulling about 5,500rpm and looked to my left to see Tiff in the blue-and-white Formula One car. It's a vision forever imprinted on my brain.

A waved flag was the cue to hit our respective throttles hard and even though the M5 is a saloon car with supercar qualities, Tiff was so quick that he left me like a bullet from a gun. His car went off with an ear-piercing scream that ripped through my helmet-muffled ears. It made a mockery of my 200mph motor as he shot off, grabbing three gears within the space of about 30 metres. When Tiff could speak, all he could breathe were the words: "Stunning.

Phenomenal. Violent." Lucky boy! After one lap his neck muscles "had gone" and by lap two, so too had his brain.

Back in the M5, I was driving as hard and as fast as I could, with the rear tyres smoking round each corner as I tried (but failed) to keep it as smooth as possible. With so much power and such urgency in the situation, the back end slid out of line really easily. Although it looked and felt fantastic, it's not the quickest way round a bend. I was getting hot and sweaty with the effort of wringing every last drop of speed from it, and although it did a first-class job, it was no match for the F1 car. Tiff reeled me in after three laps – 5.7 miles – while I had done just two. My average lap speed had been 74mph, which would have been quick enough to put me in the middle of a British Touring Car race, but Tiff's 102mph average was unsurpassable. A truly magical day.

THE FACTS

Engine: 5.0-litre V10 (M5), V10 (F1)

Performance: 0–62 mph
in 4.7 seconds, 200mph+ (M5)
0–62 mph in the blink of
an eye, 200mph+ (F1)

Price: £67,300 (M5),
£priceless (F1)

38. ASTON MARTIN ONE-77

A couple of statistics for you here. The world's population is somewhere in the region of seven billion, and Aston Martin will make just 77 of its super-duper supercar, the One-77. So, the chances of you owning one are even more unlikely than winning the Lottery. And the likelihood of that, fact-lovers, is one in 14 million. And that's before you even think about the not-so small matter of the car's price: £1.2 million, which would rule out most of us non-jackpot winners anyway.

Aston's One-77 (pronounced *one seven seven*) is not only the most expensive production car to wear the company's wings, but also the most handsome. Its hand-crafted aluminium bodywork is perfectly proportioned, despite a rear end curvaceous enough to have me wobbling on a treadmill for a very long time.

But this big backside is what defines the car as a pure muscle machine, hinting at its abilities to flatten the most demanding bends. There are also some gentle, lighter strokes of the designer's pen which convey a sense of speed, so it looks fast when static, but they also let you know this can be as fast as lightning on the move.

The car has only been driven by the development team as I write, but it's the most exquisite piece of motoring haute-couture and sits very near the top of my "must have" list. The test drivers are no slouches because they've managed to stretch the One-77's legs all the way to 220mph and that puts it into the elite 200mph+ club, whose members include the Bugatti Veyron, Ferrari 458 and Lamborghini Murcielago.

Under that sensationally sculpted bonnet and behind the designer grille is a whopping 7.3-litre V12 engine with a mouth-watering 700bhp. These juicy numbers are translated into miles via a new six-speed gearbox with column-mounted paddles behind the steering wheel. They then make their merry way to the 20-inch rear alloys, wrapped in specially-developed low-profile Pirelli P Zero rubber and onto the road. Here, the tyres have the potential to leave the naughtiest layer of evidence should your right foot become a little too heavy, officer.

Aston says this British-built motor is its definitive sports car, combining hand-built craftsmanship with high-tech materials and methods. Beneath its beautiful body is a carbon fibre monocoque that's lightweight and immensely rigid. Then there's the suspension, that not only features a few world-firsts for a road car – including Dynamic Suspension Spool Valve technology – but it can also be tailored to suit the driving styles of each of the 77 owners. This will be done by Aston's engineers, who can set each car up to be the ultimate long-distance GT motor or a machine that will be perfectly at home doing hot laps of the Nürburgring.

Ensuring high speeds are dramatically slashed on the way into slow tricky corners on the track or road are a set of carbon ceramic brakes that can withstand much higher temperatures than traditional metal ones. But no matter what speed the One-77's at, I can think of at least 77 reasons to want one.

ABOVE: This car should come with a rule: if you're not dressed to thrill, you can't come in. It's so gorgeous it leaves me drooling like a rabid dog.

THE FACTS

Engine: 7.3-litre V12

Performance: 0–60 mph in 3.5 seconds, 220mph

Price: £1,200,000 approx

37. ASTON MARTIN VANQUISH S

This car is one big hunk of love! The Aston Martin Vanquish S was at one time the fastest road-going car in the history of the marquee and it could top 200mph. With its chiselled features and a fuel tank full of testosterone, it was very much the Alpha male of the Aston pack. It was regarded as the car the company wanted to build, rather than the one that it had to in order to keep cash ringing through the tills.

"… Aston Martin sent a man to our remote location – via helicopter."

It reworked the DB7's 6.0-litre V12 engine to give more power – 520bhp – and it'll pounce to 62mph in 4.6 seconds. Its magical top speed is a figure only a small percentage of people have ever seen, so I decided to authenticate Aston's claim and film it for *Fifth Gear*.

A passing interest in maths was the only qualification required to calculate we'd need a fairly straight piece of road and not too much of a headwind to bag our booty. So, a disused airfield in Norfolk was booked, with a lengthy two-and-a-half miles that should be enough to hit the number that had eluded me all my life. Happy days.

At 9am, we'd already had an hour's worth of filming statics in the can. Next came my first piece to camera, after which the plan was to jump in the car and do a massive power slide to exit the frame. So I said my bit, slipped into the big leather seat, turned the steering wheel full lock to the left and unleashed its 520bhp in one deft dollop. The V12 snarled in appreciation, the cameras were rolling, I was grinning. I yanked my foot off the clutch and then … I went nowhere.

Like Poirot looking for clues, I buried my head under the bonnet and saw a belt hanging lose. The force of the full power combined with the acute angle I was asking the car to drive off at had been too much. Before you think I was being overly hard on the Vanquish, I wasn't: this is a move I've done in every rear-wheel-drive car I've ever driven, because it's fun.

We called Aston Martin, who sent a man to our remote location – via helicopter. It was a magnificent sight and the director lined up a shot with it coming in to land behind me while I said, "Now that's what I call service."

Unfortunately the same thing happened again before we finally got to concentrate on the 200mph straight-line run. I accelerated from 0 to 100mph in 9.8 seconds (matching Aston's figures) and urged the V12 through second gear, third, fourth and fifth. At 168mph, the revs hit 7,000rpm and I changed up into its final gear and kept the throttle buried. 170, 174 … but the end of the road was approaching faster than my target speed. So, at 178.06mph, I had to jump on the brakes and call it quits. Not such happy days. We worked out the car would need a further two miles to add those precious 22mph to its speed, proving it's one thing to own a 200mph car, and quite another to reach it.

LEFT: Just like Bentley's Speed, this big bruiser of an Aston needs a lot of room to reach its top whack. But it's jolly good fun trying.

THE FACTS

Engine: 6.0-litre V12

Performance: 0–62 mph in 4.6 seconds, 178.5mph (but Aston claims 204mph)

Price: £160,000

36. MASERATI TROFEO

On July 11, 2004, I became the first woman to win a Maserati race in the history of the Italian manufacturer. It's one of the things I'm most proud of.

It was at Silverstone during the weekend of the British Formula One Grand Prix and I was racing in the Maserati Trofeo championship for identical V8-powered Coupé Cambiocorsa cars. The series raced throughout the year in five countries at high-profile events and almost 30 cars battled against each other for top honours. The Trofeo was launched the year before and the prototype cars had been tested by Ferrari's then-F1 star, Michael Schumacher, and the team's test driver, Luca Badoer.

The cars were specially-developed at Maserati's Modena factory in Italy and were based on the road-going £60,000 four-seater Coupé, but they weighed less and went faster than their road-going sibling. The heavy air-conditioning system was taken out, as was the sound-proofing, sound system and other non-essentials to make way for a race seat, roll-over cage and 18-inch wheels with Pirelli slick tyres. An upgraded brake system and race-ready dampers and springs were only mechanical changes. Under the bonnet was a 4.2-litre V8 with 413bhp that went to the rear wheels, and on top of these an impressive rear wing to help aerodynamics.

My race was classed an endurance one (not a 20-minute sprint), so the rules required two drivers to share the time. I was paired with the experienced Porsche 911 racer Matthew Marsh, whom I'd raced against years previously in Caterhams. Neither of us had raced the Maserati before, whereas others on the grid were regulars. Matthew had more racing experience than me and was therefore a little quicker, so he set our best qualifying time which saw us start up in the first third of the grid. We were very happy.

Matthew started the race in our Zegna-backed black-and-white car, with our names across the top of the windscreen. This is never the most relaxing time for the driver who's left watching from the garage, but after about 25 minutes of incident-free racing, Matthew drove into the pits for the swap. He'd managed to gain a couple of places so tensions were high for the perfect and super-fast change-over and my nerves cranked themselves up.

Off I roared to join the race, relishing the fact that the Maserati was so much fun and not at all intimidating to drive quickly. We were racing on the 3.2-miles long Grand Prix track – the same one that the likes of Michael Schumacher would be on later in the day – and I caught and passed a couple of cars early in my session which was terrific. But all too soon there was a big shunt and the race was stopped. The officials declared the results at a point in the race where Matthew and I had been leading, and so we were the winners, even though we didn't cross the finish line and take the chequered flag.

As I stood on the top step of the podium (where Schumacher would later stand) and heard the British National anthem play for us, I cried. I was moved again to be given our winners' trophies by the first Formula One woman driver: Maria Teresa de Filippis, who drove a Maserati in the 1958 Monaco GP.

"Off I roared to the race, relishing the fact the Maserati was so much fun..."

ABOVE: Each time I see this picture my insides erupt with joy because it was one of the most thrilling days of my life. I shall be grateful forever to Matthew Marsh for helping us reach the top.

THE FACTS

Engine: 4.2-litre V8

Performance: 0–60mph in sub-five seconds, 170mph+

Price: £120,000 plus taxes for an "arrive and drive" package

35. ASTON MARTIN V8 VANTAGE
34. ASTON MARTIN DBS

Power, beauty and soul are the three most important elements at Aston Martin and the DB9 embodies them all. Launched in 2003 as the successor to the DB7, it is the epitome of Britishness, despite being wrapped in a GT sports coupé coat rather than a tweed jacket.

ABOVE: Vantage clearly has one of the best tailors in the world with nips and tucks in all the right places.
RIGHT: The DBS broke the world record for the most barrel rolls assisted by a cannon in the Bond film. Seven in total.

"Think Jude Law, with the punch of Ricky Hatton."

But its little brother, the Vantage, has nestled its way into my affections mainly due to its perfectly-tailored body. Its aluminium panels and rear steel wings drip toward the 19-inch alloys like melted choccy off a spoon and its chrome-surround windows give a designer sparkle.

You'd be forgiven for thinking it a bit fragile because it's a surprisingly petite car, but its achingly pretty looks do a brilliant job of keeping its Porsche 911-challenging performance under tight wraps. Think Jude Law, with the punch of Ricky Hatton.

When it comes to signing on the dotted line, you have a choice of two engines – a 4.7-litre V8 with 420bhp or, if that's not thirsty enough for you, there's a 6.0-litre V12, producing 510bhp. No matter which one you go for, you're guaranteed a movie soundtrack on every journey. Both are sensationally sonorous and you'll find that you never want to fill that passenger seat.

The V8 devours the revs in all six gears, though its peak power comes in at 7,000rpm and it greedily tucks into miles of tarmac in a rapid amount of time. Every type of road is its best friend, but B-roads are its very best. As soon as the hedgerows start to zigzag, the Vantage flexes its haunches and shows why it's been the only real alternative in years to Porsche's unflappable 911.

It tackles the twists almost as beautifully as it looks, its snout staying glued to whatever line you've picked, thanks to endless grip from the front tyres. If you need a little adjustment mid-bend, it reassuringly responds and tucks in a bit more.

If you want to mark your territory as you exit, a hearty dollop of throttle and a careful juggle of the steering allows the rear end to autograph the road for followers to admire. When you begin to really hustle the Vantage it starts to slip behind the talented 911 S, but the gap is more of a sliver than a stream. Its minor faults only come to light because the 911 is just so darned brilliant at responding to your slightest thoughts and it rewards by sending back the most detailed information that will saturate the most insatiably demanding driver.

I can't end the Vantage story without mentioning Aston Martin's new flagship, the DBS V12 that James Bond ragged and rolled in *Casino Royale*. It's a big, bold, brassy motor befitting such a beef cake. Aston's 510bhp 5.9-litre V12 make this car an expensive way into the brand – £166,872 for the Coupé and an additional £9,000 for the Volante version.

THE FACTS

Engine: 4.7-litre V8 (V8), 6.0-litre V12 (V12)
5.9-litre V12 (DBS)

Performance: 0–60 mph in 4.7 seconds, 178mph (V8), 4.1 seconds, 190mph (V12), 4.2 seconds, 191mph (DBS)

Price: £89,000 (V8 Vantage)
£135,000 (V12 Vantage)

33. PORSCHE PANAMERA TURBO

Porsche's first foray into the four-seater, four-door supersaloon market received as much bad press for its unattractive looks as the Cayenne SUV had done a few years earlier. Admittedly it looks as though someone took a Cayenne and trod on it, but the Panamera's unconventional shape has always appealed to me and I admire the designers for not making any dead-straight lines on the car – even the rear glass is angled so it's wider at the top than at the bottom and this nicely accentuates its curvy backside.

"… an astonishing bit of physics for a car that's longer than a Ford Transit."

I drove it at the launch in 2009 at Porsche's Silverstone-based track, which has all the right ingredients of undulations and twists to emulate the best a B-road can offer. There I tested the three initial models (more will join the range), which include the £73,000 rear-drive S version that's actually my favourite because its chassis is the most simple, offering instant old-fashioned oversteer whenever you ask for it. Then there's the £79,000 4S version, which has the same 4.8-litre V8 with 400bhp, but with a less-intimidating four-wheel-drive system. The all-singing £97,000 Turbo cranks the power up to 500bhp, sits on 20-inch alloy wheels and has a rear spoiler that pops up and spreads out across its tail in one neat move.

Inside, there's the most striking centre console running the length of the cabin and it's packed with well-defined buttons that feel as good as they look. The perfectly-sculpted driver's seat is exactly the same as the two in back and this is an important detail because Porsche reckon the Panamera will be very popular with people who have a chauffeur on speed dial. There's plenty of knee room in the back as well as height because the seats are as low down as physically possible and the roofline remains high over your head before it slopes down to join the rear bumper.

But back in the only chair I'll ever want to be in, I was amazed at how the car shrank around me as I took to the track – so much so that I had to check my rear-view mirror to make sure I wasn't in a 911.

The steering is beautifully weighted and the four-wheel-drive chassis allows you to get the power down early in the corner, with lots of grip and grunt ever-ready to fire you out. If you opt for the extra £1,900 Chrono Package, you get a couple of hardcore suspension modes which beef things up further for harder track work. You also have the option to turn the traction control system off, which turns this 4WD car into more of a rear-drive machine where the back end slips and slides perfectly – an astonishing bit of physics for a car that's longer than a Ford Transit. You'll also get a built-in stopwatch to time your track day laps. Or the school run. The Panamera is more involving than all of its rivals to date, but looks set for an almighty lifelong battle with Aston Martin's Rapide.

LEFT: This car is as long as the manufacturer's name above my head but the Panamera feels as small as the "P" when you drive it in anger.

THE FACTS

Engine: 4.8-litre V8

Performance: 0–62mph in 4.2 seconds, 188mph

Price: £97,358

32. PORSCHE BOXSTER

When Porsche first launched this two-seater sports car in the mid-1990s it was the company's first new offering for almost two decades. As a 911 devotee I was seriously concerned that this new smaller, cheaper car would somehow carry the tag of a poor man's 911, and maybe even start to weaken the brand, but those thoughts went straight out of my head the moment I slipped into the perfectly-designed cabin.

"It's also got a really supple ride to make it a great all-round driver's car."

The Germans know how to make interiors work and here was no exception. Tightly-stitched leather, creative dials that overlap and neat rows of buttons were reminiscent of the 911's interior, and that's certainly no bad thing. Outside, its elegant and simple curves give it a shape that appeals to almost everyone and the electric hood can be dropped in about 12 seconds, which adds to its appeal and practicality as an everyday roadster.

Mid-mounted behind the seats, its first engine was a 2.5-litre straight-six with just over 200bhp and a 0–60mph time of 6.5 seconds – all very healthy numbers, but the rear-drive chassis could cope with much, much more. Today's most potent version is a 3.4-litre with 315bhp and the chassis has evolved brilliantly though it could still take a bit more.

All the engines have shared the same characteristics in that they have great bottom-end pull and are really smooth to the red line. The manual gearboxes have a delightful springiness and the semi-automatic Tiptronic systems with finger-tip controls on the steering wheel give even faster changes but leave you a little removed from the action. The Boxster is without doubt more user-friendly than a 911, and it's always been the best-performing roadster for the money whenever I've tested it for car magazines or for *Fifth Gear*.

I love driving them as they offer so much for a car that's relatively small. It's great for pottering around town and yet utterly fabulous when you give it its head and let the chassis wind its way through a series of twists. Incredibly surefooted, it has a reassuring level of grip as it squats down to the road and surges onward. The steering is so alert as well that you always feel part of the process. It's also got a really supple ride to make it a great all-round driver's car.

In 2010 Porsche brought out the most hard-core and lightweight version yet, the Boxster Spyder. The 3.4-litre has a tiny bit more power at 320bhp but it's managed to shed 80kg, which boosts its 0–62mph time from 5.3 seconds to 5.1. I drove it at Porsche's purpose-built handling circuit at Silverstone and spent the day sliding the rear end round the corners and then racing on to the next. The weight-saving strip of material for the manual roof is fiddly to put on and Porsche recommends you keep below 124mph with it in place for safety reasons, which is way short of the car's 164mph maximum. It costs £4,000 more than the already-brilliant 3.4 S, but is perfect for sunny track days.

ABOVE: Few things in life make me happier than when I have the tail hanging out on a car and here the Spyder was very willing to oblige. Those lovely rubber marks on the track are all mine. Tee hee.

THE FACTS

Engine: from 2.9-litre to 3.4-litre flat-six

Performance: 0–60mph from 5.1 seconds, 163mph to 5.9 seconds, 170mph

Price: From £34,996 to £46,063 (latest)

31. PAGANI ZONDA

If you're going to make an exotic Italian supercar then you're best off giving it a name that conjures up magic, intrigue and romance – which the Pagani Zonda does by the bucket load. It sits in the Premier League of supercars and is headed by a former Lamborghini employee, Horacio Pagani – an Argentinian who found his soul was a perfect match for car-crazy Italy, where he set up his supercar operation.

"Surely a mobile masterpiece."

The car is unbelievably stunning. Its scoops and swoops, and wings and quadruple exhaust pipes make it look more like a spaceship than a road car, and the closer you look the more detail you notice. This is a real labour of love that's had an exquisite amount of attention lavished on the smallest parts and with motorsport precision.

Open up the rear end of the car like a clam shell and it reveals another work of art in the engine bay. Shiny struts and carbon-fibre body parts encase a 7.3-litre V12 Mercedes-Benz engine with 555bhp. Such a mix of skill and beauty makes you feel dizzy just standing near it. Its performance is enough to earn it a place at the high table with the McLaren F1, Porsche Carrera GT and Bugatti EB 110. It'll hit 100mph in a little over seven seconds and won't stop until it's seen 220mph.

In 2002 the car cost £298,000, but if you had a bit more cash to splash and could wait a couple of years, then the even more striking Zonda Roadster would fit the bill for £383,000. Surely a mobile masterpiece. I flew to Pagani's HQ to meet the boss and relieve him of a Zonda Roadster for a few hours. Mr Pagani is very much a hands-on owner, as he helped me remove the glass roof and store it in the nose of the car in a specially-designed compartment.

It's slightly intimidating to walk up to a car that's so breathtaking, and so with eyes wide and jaw slack, I stumbled into the cockpit which itself was like sitting in an art gallery jammed full of masterpieces. There's carbon fibre that's been made into the most unlikely shapes of two roll-over hoops above the seats and then there's aluminium that's been machined into the most delightful switches and buttons, and to remind you where you are, the word "Roadster" is autographed into the dash. Then there's the thousand shades of silver paint to choose

LEFT: The Zonda is a proper piece of exotica and you just know that if Pagani designed a humble shoe lace it would be the most exquisite in the world.

from, even colours that have yet to be invented, and the endless list of interior trim options: baby-yellow ostrich leather in my test car. Michelin even make a special set of tyres for it. My favourite features, though, are the door mirrors that sit high on the A-pillars and look like wasp antennae with their slender stalks.

Out on the Italian country roads the Zonda Roadster felt overly wide, but its sensational looks do a great job in getting people to move out of your way. The clutch was on the heavy side, the gearbox beefy, but with a well-oiled feel to it, the brakes really firm and the steering was truly special. The wheel itself was chunky but it managed to offer a delicate feel to the front tyres and as such, had such an accurate turn-in. Then there was the noise, which was made even more glorious without the roof. A glorious car to back up the name.

THE FACTS

Engine: 7.3-litre V12

Performance: 0–60mph in 3.7 seconds, 220mph

Price: £383,000

30. NISSAN 350Z

29. NISSAN 370Z

28. MITSUBIS

27. MCL

26.

NI EVO

REN MP4-12C

MCLAREN SLR

25. HONDA NSX

24. FORD ESCORT RS COSWORTH

23. BMW M3

22. BMW M3 CABRIO

21. BMW M3 CSL

30. NISSAN 350Z

29. NISSAN 370Z

This car is a little gem of a machine that never received the public profile I always thought it deserved. The Nissan 350Z burst onto the sports coupé market in the first half of the new millennium and became one of my all-time favourites. Available with a convertible hood as well, it carried the Japanese manufacturer's Z-car brand to dizzy heights of brilliance.

"The engine is incredibly gutsy but it delivers its punch in a velvety way ..."

It may not be the most drop-dead gorgeous piece of metal you'll ever see but it's a car that instantly engages you the moment you turn the key to the 3.5-litre V6. It's all muscle, this motor, with 276bhp (at launch) that is more than enough to get the back end sliding off the line in a hurried take-off, reaching 60mph in under 6.0 seconds. The engine is incredibly gutsy but delivers its punch in a velvety way, from the lightest of throttle touches to the most demanding. From the bottom of the rev range to the top, the grunt is always on hand to get you down the road that little bit quicker.

It's perfectly matched to one of the best rear-drive chassis in the world, too. Turn the traction control off and the back end steps out with amazing control and composure until you straighten up and grow up. I have spent many blissful hours on race circuits in road-going 350Zs doing one-handed slides and remain in awe of the Nissan engineers who created such a work of genius. It really rewards the keen driver. Then there's the ride, which is the perfect alliance of being supple over undulating roads and firm enough to attack tight turns, making it a wonderful companion on all journeys.

In 2009, the 350Z was superseded by the 370Z, which wears a tighter, sharper suit and a bigger 3.7-litre V6 engine with 322bhp, as well as an asking price from £28,000. That gives the entry-level BMW Z4 and Porsche Cayman a serious cause for concern, particularly as they are both under-powered by comparison too.

ABOVE: The 350Z is one of the few cars that I recommended the most when people ask me what sportscar to buy. Its chassis is made from my dreams.

The 370Z appeals to the wallet as much as the enthusiast because this new car has lost very little of the 350Z's charisma. It is a little more mature in its handling but it has the best boy racer gadget that's ever been fitted to a manual gearbox, and that's something Nissan calls Synchro Rev Control. It's an automatic blipper for the throttle so when you change down from fourth to third, or third to second for example, the revs 'blip' and rise to meet the needs of the incoming gear. It's heel-and-toe downshifts for the lazy, and it's only ever been on racy automatics before now. I really enjoy both new and old cars but it's the hairy-chested performance and thrills of the 350Z that will remain my favourite.

THE FACTS

Engine: 3.5-litre V6 (350Z),
3.7-litre V6 (370Z)

Performance: 0–60mph in sub 6.0 seconds,
155mph (350Z),
0–62mph in 5.3 seconds,
155mph (370Z)

Price: £26,000 (350Z), £28,345 (370Z)

28. MITSUBISHI EVO

The Mitsubishi Evo is one of the closest experiences we mortals can get to driving a world rally car – for a fraction of the price. The Evo VI (six) was the first Lancer Evo to be officially sold in the UK and once I'd tested it for BBC's *Top Gear* back in 1999, it became a firm favourite. One year previously the car, albeit in rally trim, took Tommi Makinen to World Championship glory. His car's clever "active yaw control" is present in the showroom version, using sensors to monitor the steering, throttle, brakes and g-forces. These then do their best to eliminate understeer or oversteer, which both hinder fast progress.

"The power comes in such a rush that you have to be ready before you ask for it ..."

I ts four-wheel-drive system does a great job in maintaining traction as well and helps to dish out the 276bhp to all four wheels, when necessary. Under the vented bonnet is a 2.0-litre turbocharged engine, which can hit 60mph in 4.4 seconds. When I drove the car on a disused tarmac airfield it was pouring with rain, but it still shot off the line to hit 60mph and come back to a standstill within nine seconds.

The power comes in such a rush that you have to be ready before you ask for it, especially round corners, because it has the grip to match its full force. The steering, brakes and five-speed gearbox are some of the sharpest, crispest and most rewarding controls I've ever tested. It's not what you'd call a beautiful-looking machine, but it'll definitely attract your attention just as it caught the eye of Subaru's Impreza, which instantly became this car's arch rival.

Almost ten years and quite a few Evo derivatives later, I tested the Evo VI against the latest version at the time, the Evo IX (nine) FQ320, in a shoot-out at the Anglesey race track in Wales. I'm pretty sure the FQ stood for something like "very quick" because it was particularly speedy at going sideways, even if its straight-line performance wasn't much improved on the Evo VI with 0–62mph taking 4.5 seconds. Which just goes to show how ace the VI was. Even more so when you realize the new car was powered by a 2.0-litre turbocharged engine with more power at 326bhp.

The newer car had even more electronic wizardry, allowing the driver to set the car up for tarmac, gravel or snow roads, and even though its transmission, steering and brakes were as fantastically accurate and beefy as the older car, its set-up was a bit softer which helped it to be so tail-happy. This was to be the Evo IX's downfall though, because it lost 1/4 of a second over the course of a lap to the tidier Evo VI, proving evolution isn't always an improvement.

THE FACTS

Engine: 2.0-litre turbocharged

Performance: 0–60mph from 4.1 seconds, 155mph

Price: From £30,759 (latest)

LEFT: This picture looks a little odd because it was captured from a TV camera as we shot the Mitsubishi for *Fifth Gear*. **ABOVE:** For anyone who cares, my T-shirt has the words from a Duran Duran song in it.

27. MCLAREN MP4-12C

26. MERCEDES-BENZ SLR MCLAREN

It's a monumentally exciting time when a manufacturer tells the world that it's all set to build the next supercar. The sense of anticipation grows exponentially when the announcement comes from the newly-formed McLaren Automotive company, which can count two Formula-One World Champions as test drivers.

cLaren boss Ron Dennis recently took a back seat from the Formula One side of the business to set up and concentrate on the road car department. Although this MP4-12C is the fourth street-legal car that McLaren has been involved with, it's the first one to be totally built in-house. This includes the 3.8-litre twin-turbocharged V8 engine with 600bhp. Then there's the seven-speed double-clutch sequential transmission and the promise of reaching 60mph in three seconds and on to over 200mph. It's one of the greenest supercars too.

Launched in early spring 2010 by Jenson Button and Lewis Hamilton, McLaren's F1 superstars, these chaps were two of just a select few who'd driven the car. Both declared it to be really great, as you'd expect from employees on the payroll. But I'll bet it's actually more than great because Ron Dennis wouldn't sign off anything short of perfect.

To look at the MP4-12C reminds me of the McLaren F1 supercar, with its soft edges and rounded body. It contrasts surprisingly with Ferrari's 458 Italia and Lamborghini's Gallardo, with their sharp angles and "look at me" designs. The driver is very much the focus of this new car, though, with the development concept being "designed around the driver".

Unlike the McLaren F1 road car, this is a two-seater with a much cheaper price tag of around £150,000. There are plans to make 1,000 in the first year, which will hopefully start to turn a profit in the fourth year, so we can expect to see many, many more of these than we did of the super-exclusive F1. McLaren Automotive will establish 35 retail outlets in 19 countries, where customers can spec-up their MP4-12C from a diverse list of interior trims, as well as adding lightweight sports exhausts, carbon ceramic brakes, a voice-activated sat-nav or even a carbon-fibre engine cover.

ABOVE: The MP4-12C is one of the most hotly anticipated cars of 2010 and the company hopes it'll be even more successful than the highly acclaimed SLR.

As the world welcomes a new supercar, it waves goodbye to an old one the Mercedes-Benz SLR McLaren. This was the love child of a joint venture when the German manufacturer held a large stake in the English motorsport-focused company. The SLR was the flagship Benz and it stood for Sport, Light, Racing. Available as a coupé and a roadster, they are instantly recognizable by their enormously long noses. The best one I saw was a sensationally smart matt black one as it thrashed round Oulton Park circuit on a track day. Gorgeous.

Under that bonnet is a 5.4-litre supercharged V8 engine, hand-built, of course, with 617bhp, which will punch you forward at the slightest stab of the throttle. Its five-speed automatic transmission is great for town work and when you're ready for the drive of your life it's best to use the wheel-mounted gear-changes so you can hang onto the revs for as long as you need in each gear.

The entire body is made from carbon fibre to keep the weight down and the speed up. It'll hit 62mph in 3.7 seconds and go on past 200mph. Its doors are another interesting feature as they open upward and then forward, but this movement isn't as graceful as the true gullwing doors of the Mercedes-Benz SLS AMG. It's still a very fine motor car, though.

"... the development concept being 'designed around the driver'."

THE FACTS

Engine: 4.7-litre V8

Performance: 0–62mph in 5.3 seconds, 176mph

Price: £96,175

25. HONDA NSX

Honda's NSX was the first supercar that you could really use every day for your commute, or even for taking one lucky school child to school. This strict two-seater was a celebration of Honda's Formula One success. Although the NSX carried high-tech F1 know-how, it also came with the Japanese manufacturer's renowned reliability so you could leave the car in your garage for many, many weeks and return to fire it up at the first turn of the key. A Formula One car is a lot less reliable, and so too were this car's supercar rivals in the 1990s. The NSX was so good in this respect that it topped a customer reliability survey in 1990.

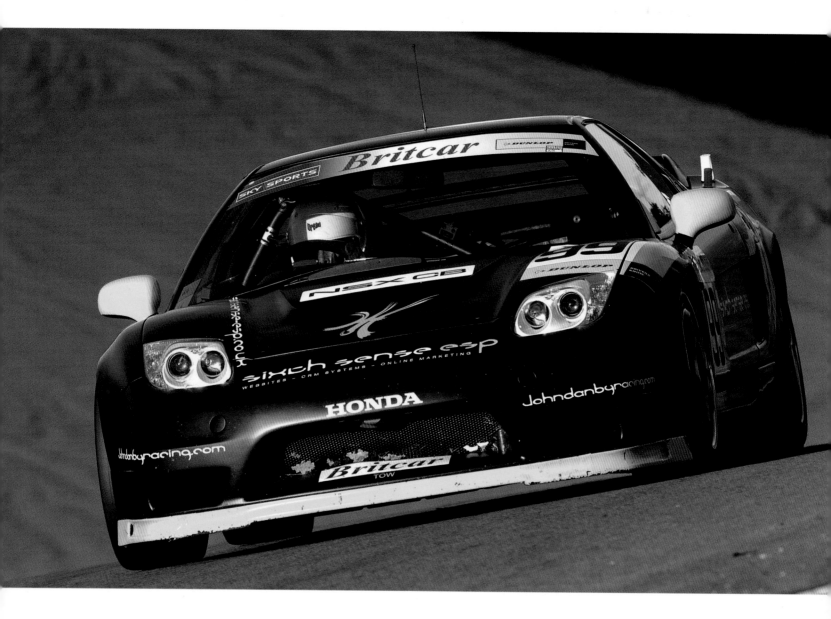

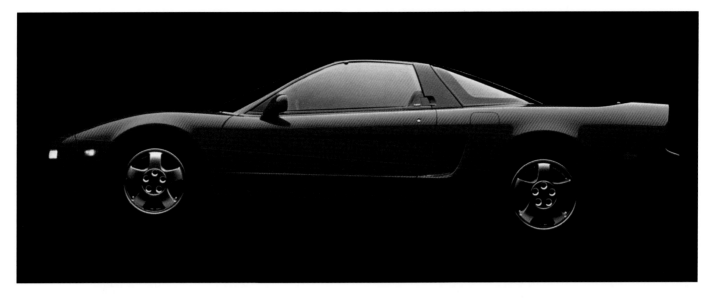

"... I would be very happy for my gran to have a potter about in it."

It also had some special magic about it, thanks to one of the world's most talented and famous Formula One drivers, who was involved in its development. If the handling was good enough for one Ayrton Senna to sign off on, then it's plenty good enough for us mere mortals. Even Gordon Murray, the McLaren F1 designer, owned a NSX and drew inspiration from it for his supercar.

Everything about the NSX's handling is immediate. Once you've slithered your way into the snug and supportive leather seat, you can feel each ripple and rut of the road through the steering. It's alive and direct, and as close to Ayrton's F1 car as I'm sure he could safely make it. You sit low to the ground and the rear-drive chassis responds instantly, yet it's not intimidating as other supercars can be. It may be a 170mph machine that can hit 62mph in 5.5 seconds, but I would be happy for my gran to potter about in it.

The 3.2-litre V6 engine nestled behind the seats has Honda's VTEC technology so it loves to rev, and you can feel the point where the variable valve timing (VTEC) shifts up into its banzai mode and the full 280bhp is all yours to play with. The slender, all-aluminium body keeps its weight down to that of a Ford Focus. It had such a flawless design from the outset that it barely changed during its 15-year life. Its demise came about partly because increasingly demanding emission regulations meant it wasn't financially viable anymore. I had the honour of driving one of the last ones to be sold in the UK in 2004.

In 2009, I also competed in the only race-prepared NSX in the UK. It was one of the most physically-demanding cars I've ever driven because it was midway through its metamorphosis from a high-mileage road car to a racer. The power steering had been removed to save weight, but that wrenched my arms from their sockets after just a few laps, and I'm no wimp. The heavy glass remained in place, as did the manual gearbox which has a wonderfully short-shift on the road, but on a track it's overly cumbersome – trying to wrestle the steering and change gear while rapidly slowing down made for a busy race. A paddle-shift semi-automatic is thankfully in the pipeline.

It sits on slick tyres so the handling is more defined than everand even through my noise-reducing helmet the engine barked wonderfully and the revs never seemed to end. After an incredibly hard-fought 90-minute race, where I shared the driving with the car's owner, David Fenn, we finished an ecstatic third.

LEFT: Me at the wheel of a unique NSX in its first race. **ABOVE**: The best way to view this Honda is in profile – such simple lines.

THE FACTS

Engine: 3.0-litre V6

Performance: 0–60mph in 5.5 seconds, 170mph

Price: £60,000

24. FORD ESCORT RS COSWORTH

For the last two decades I have had a slightly unhealthy love affair with rear spoilers: the bigger the better. I'm not so bothered about the ones that only just poke out from the top of a boot, but I'm a sucker for those that stick out like balconies. They make me go weak at the knees. It's all because of this car, the Ford Escort RS Cosworth.

On sale from 1992 to 1996, just over 7,000 were built and I think it remains Ford's most recognizable car to date – largely thanks to that spoiler. It was so huge it had to have some sort of support to hold it up and consequently it was known as the whale tail. It's beyond fantastic.

The first 2,500 were built as part of the homologation rules for the World Rally Championship car. Then, in 1994, more were made, but with a smaller turbocharger to reduce turbo lag and make the car more user-friendly for everyday driving. With this later batch, owners could order their Cossie without the whale tail. I would never have sanctioned anything so ridiculous.

The Escort Cossie was the ultimate rude boy for the road. Its first-class looks were backed up by first-class drivers on the World Rally stage with the likes of Tommi Makinen, François Delcour, Carlos Sainz, Malcolm Wilson, Ari Vatanen, Stiq Blomqvist and Miki Biasion. The car never managed to bag a WRC title though, despite individual rally wins, which is a crying shame.

Ford has a wonderful heritage department where, among other immaculate old motors, is a low-mileage Escort Cosworth that I got to drive for *Fifth Gear* at Anglesey racing circuit. Boy, oh boy did it bring back memories of when I drove the car in its heyday! It was as agile and rewarding as the ones I'd driven almost 15 years before.

Its four-wheel-drive system sets its handling limits pretty high, so you can go round corners much more quickly than you'd first judge. Throw it into a bend, plant the throttle as soon as you dare and just let the 4x4 system put the engine's 227bhp onto the tarmac and pull you through. It's amazingly competent and can make inadequate drivers feel like heroes.

The steering and brakes were as sharp as ever and even the leather-clad sports seats were plump and pert. Driving it against the clock, against a much more youthful and heavier Ford Focus RS with a similar-size engine and power, the Escort Cossie did me proud and beat the young whipper snapper by almost one and a half seconds. Not bad at all around the 1.55-mile undulating track. It felt smoother too and was in its element when its whale tail was swinging about. Me too. I still love it.

LEFT: At Anglesey with a cheesy grin because I'm so close to that fabulous tail. Next to the Cossie is the Focus RS, beaten into second place round the track.

THE FACTS

Engine: 2.0-litre four-cylinder

Performance: 0–60mph in 6.2 seconds, 140mph

Price: £25,000

23. BMW M3

22. BMW M3 CABRIO

21. BMW M3 CSL

I start salivating as soon as I see even a hint of the original M3's bulging wheel arches – undoubtedly its most striking features. Launched in 1986, it was from BMW's motorsport division, and filled the racy gap left by the M1. It was more practical, though, because it was based on the medium-sized 3-series so it came with rear seats and a boot, though it was only on sale as a left hooker.

"... there's an aura about the car makes you want to stay put."

Perched on top of the shortened boot was a spoiler that looked as though it would actually keep the tail down at high speeds rather than just look good. It did the latter too, though. A 2.3-litre four-cylinder engine pumped petrol round its veins, with 200bhp going to the rear 15-inch wheels. They seem tiny compared to the 19-inch tyres on the most current M3. The original's distinctive flared arches were designed to fit even smaller, 10-inch wheels in full racing trim, however. It had a five-speed manual gearbox with a dog-leg first, and in road-going form, hit 60mph in 7.0 seconds with a top speed of 147mph. Tweaked suspension and sharpened steering made its handling dynamite.

Sitting in the sports seats, there's an aura about the car that makes you want to stay put, so it's just as well that it's a good-looking place to be. The dash is angled toward the driver, the controls clearly displayed. The most sought-after model was the limited-edition M3 Evolution, which arrived in 1988 and had even more power. There was also a M3 cabriolet that proved so popular it started the trend for topless versions ever since.

It's the modern, £56,000 M3 cabrio which is my current title holder for the only car you'll ever need, though, thanks to a stunning display of stylish practicality that has yet to be beaten. I had one for a weekend and needed to buy two eight-feet tall trees and transport them back home, six miles away. So I just dropped the car's top, planted the greenery in the back and mission accomplished. It looked an odd sight, definitely, but it proved that the M3 Cab is not just a show-off motor. And on top of that, the rear-drive chassis and 4.0-litre V8 are a sublime combination.

I can't miss mentioning the £58,455 M3 CSL. Launched in 2003, with a limited run of 500, it was one of the most extreme M3s ever. The Coupé Sport Lightweight (CSL) had an extra 17bhp over the M3 of its day and it was also 185kg lighter (including a carbon-fibre roof). Surprisingly this didn't make much of an impact on its 0–62mph time – 4.9 seconds – but the way it handled was stupefying.

Its 19-inch rims were wrapped in special rubber that relished a racing circuit and the car was much more at home at Silverstone than the high street. I spent a day there with a CSL giving sideways passenger rides and had to be dragged out of it at the close of play. I loved it. It was amazingly rewarding in every aspect and impeccably engineered, as well as the stuff dreams are made of. Pricey, though, at nearly £60,000, which was almost £20,000 more than the M3.

ABOVE/LEFT: I know it's greedy, but I could justify owning all three at the same time. Easily. If push came to shove and I could have just one, I'd take the CSL.

THE FACTS

Engine: 2.3-litre four-cylinder (original), 4.0-litre V8, (cabriolet), 3.2-litre six-cylinder (CSL)

Performance: 0–60 mph in 7.0seconds, 147mph (original); 0–60 mph in 5.3 seconds, 155mph (cabriolet); 0–60 mph in 4.9 seconds, 155mph (CSL)

Price: £53,275 (original), £57,285 (cabriolet), £58,455 (CSL)

20. LANCIA DELTA INTE[GRALE]

19. MCLAREN F1

18. LAMBORG[HINI]

17. FERR[ARI]

16.

RALE HF TURBO

INI GALLARDO

RI 458 ITALIA

ERRARI F40

15. FERRARI ENZO

14. FERRARI F50

13. BENTLEY CONTINENTAL FLYING SPUR

12. AUDI R8

11. AUDI QUATTRO

20. LANCIA DELTA INTEGRALE HF TURBO

This Lancia is very special. It formed the basis of the car that, in effect, became the successor to the Audi Quattro in the World Rally Championship stakes. When it was introduced in the second half of the 1980s, the Integrale won four drivers' and six manufacturers' titles. It was powered by a 2.0-litre turbocharged motor that revved sweetly and sounded great, but its four-wheel-drive system was the key to its success. Lancia's new technology made it more than a match for Audi's great quattro system.

"... jumping up and down like an over-excited school girl for too long, I finally settled into the Recaro seat ..."

This flagship Delta model was available only in left-hand drive and it was so popular that Lancia built many more than the 5,000 required to meet rally homologation rules. Despite being a not-very-sexy five-door hatchback on paper, its design is iconic. It includes that flat black grille, twin spot lights and the bulging wheel arches to accommodate the 15-inch alloys. Back then, that size was the business.

Recreating the manufacturer's 0–60mph time of 6.4 seconds doesn't require much skill. Even the heaviest-footed novice could launch the car with maximum revs, let go of the clutch and still, it would set off without drama to make the time. That had a lot to do with the wheelspin-intolerant 4WD set-up. This car had been a childhood favourite of mine. I remember watching the likes of Juha Kankkunen and Miki Biasion drive them to World Championship glory. It wasn't until I was much older, in the mid-2000s, that I finally had the chance to drive one.

It was one of the most memorable drives I've ever had. I was filming it for *Fifth Gear* – I have an awful lot to thank my job for – and went into the deepest, darkest parts of Wales, which boast some of the world's most challenging roads. The Integrale belonged to an incredibly generous viewer to whom I am eternally grateful. After jumping up and down like an over-excited school girl for too long, I finally settled into the Recaro seat and burbled off to see what I had been missing all these years.

A lot. Even though it was knocking on for 20 years old, the car's responses were razor-sharp. It hugged the tight twists with astonishing energy and built up the speed in between. The more I pushed it, the more it kept giving, and its pace and ability through the long sweeping bends were awesome too. Its outstanding agility matched the traction on slippery surfaces as the weather inevitably worsened throughout the day.

The five-speed manual gearbox was still wonderfully slick and light to use, and the whole experience felt as though I was driving a car made from the smoothest silk. The heady combination of the power delivery, the handling and the surprisingly comfortable ride meant it drove its way into my dream garage right there.

LEFT: From the dust plumes in its wake to the water splashes, these pictures capture the spirit of the Intergrale in battle. A true motoring legend.

THE FACTS

Engine: 2.0-litre four-cylinder turbocharged

Performance: 0–60mph in 6.4 seconds, 130mph

Price: £14,000

19. MCLAREN F1

When anyone asks my *Fifth Gear* co-presenter Tiff Needell what his favourite car is, he says the McLaren F1. That's a wonderful accolade considering Tiff is the most experienced driver I know, having raced Formula One and Le Mans, and tested tens of thousands of cars in his time. Remember also the McLaren F1 was made around 15 years ago and clearly nothing has been produced to eclipse its perfection in his eyes.

"... no expense was spared ..."

It became the world's fastest production car on release, clocking up 240mph, and was created by the joined forces of esteemed F1 designer Gordon Murray and Peter Stevens, the highly talented race, rally and road car designer. Power was sourced from an über-powerful 6.0-litre BMW Motorsport V12 engine. Before creating it, Murray spent time studying Honda's NSX to understand how to make a supercar work for everyday use – the ethos behind his F1 road car. That, and to have a car with little weight, but big power. By Jove, I think they cracked it.

It weighs 1138kg (all current Ferraris are heavier) and produces 627bhp, with one of the most glorious sounds this side of a racing circuit. The performance figures are staggering too as it'll hit 60mph in an eye watering 3.2 seconds and will reach twice the UK's speed limit in just over 10 seconds. Obviously there are very few places where its top figure can ever be reached on public roads, but there are suitable tracks around the globe that would be worth a visit.

Apart from the car's astonishing numbers, its most unusual feature is its three-seater interior, where the driver sits slap-bang in the middle and slightly ahead of the passengers. The lever for the six-speed gearbox rests just to your right and there are fewer switches on the dash than you'd find in today's most humdrum family car, so this lack of clutter lets your immediate vision focus on the job in hand.

The car was very much the star, although no expense was spared in certain areas; the engine bay behind you was lined with gold insulation. Once you owned the car, you had access to a McLaren engineer, who would be with you as soon as humanly possible, no

ABOVE: This car set a new standard in design and engineering for the supercar world, with racing versions competing in a variety of global championships too.

matter where in the world you were. With just over 100 ever being sold and a tally of 6,000 man hours each to build, those engineers could keep a pretty good track of where the cars were and how the owners were treating them.

An experienced driver friend of mine recently drove a McLaren F1 and questioned the myth about it being a faultless package. He said the steering was really heavy and the brakes were truly dreadful, but he was absolutely blown away by the engine's performance and noise, and how the car was still very much a challenge to drive quickly. Sounds like my kind of car.

THE FACTS

Engine: 6.1-litre V12

Performance: 0–60mph in 3.2 seconds, 240mph

Price: £540,000

18. LAMBORGHINI GALLARDO

If you want the cheapest way into Lamborghini ownership, then this is it. It'll still set you back as much as a roof over your head, at almost £151,000, but boy oh boy, will it make you feel like more like a million dollars. As well as being the most budget-friendly of Lamborghini's limited range, the Gallardo is also the smallest. It is almost a ruler's length shorter than the Murcielago, nearly three inches slimmer in width, but just over an inch taller. The Gallardo's styling is more angular too, with its long, slender headlights and acute rear end, and it will stop you in your tracks from whichever angle you look.

It was first launched in 2003 and was nick-named the "baby" Lambo but there's nothing infantile about this car, especially when its V10 engine barks into life with the suggestion of pulverizing power and raw speed. The LP560-4 is powered by a 5.2-litre V10 with 552bhp that guarantees thrills. It's very much this car's heart and soul, and it's never quiet, not even at tick over, where it burbles away with temptation. When you do take the bait, you'll be hard pushed not to test its 0–62mph time of 3.7 seconds or its 202mph top speed, if you happen to be on a test track.

But wherever you drive, I'm certain you'll become instantly addicted to the noise, which also vibrates to invigorate your internals and shake your soul. It has the same effect on passers-by, who demand you roar off into the distance, or at least give them one long rev before you go.

Its race-tuned chassis is rewarding and there shouldn't be too many spills, thanks to its four-wheel-drive system offering great levels of grip. Since the days of Audi's take-over, four-wheel-drive has been the norm for Lamborghinis, though I'll always prefer my raging bull to be rear-driven as it forces the driver to be the talented one. I think supercar owners, and all drivers actually, should invest money and time improving their own skills rather than relying on technology to get them out of trouble.

Anyway, I'm happy to report the majority of the Gallardo's power (70 per cent) is fed to the rear wheels most of the time, so the engineers have set the system up well. As soon as the conditions become tricky this then spreads forward to the front wheels for maximum traction across all four. Its ride is surprisingly comfortable for such a hard-looking car and its interior bursting with quality, quilted leather seats and beautiful buttons that are Audi-inspired and very user-friendly.

Rivals include Porsche's 911 Turbo and Ferrari's F430, but there's one thing you can be sure of with every trip in the Gallardo – it will be a dramatic one. For a real treat, there's a special-edition rear-wheel-drive manual version called the LP550-2. Just 250 have been produced to mark the retirement of Lamborghini's legendary test driver, Valentino Balboni. It has a tiny bit less power, but is lighter. Where do I sign?

"… the noise vibrates to invigorate your internals and shake your soul."

LEFT: A glamorous arrival to two not so glamorous settings ready to film for Fifth Gear in London in 2008, and in 2010 (**ABOVE**).

THE FACTS

Engine: 5.2-litre V10

Performance: 0–62mph in 3.7 seconds, 202mph

Price: From £150,921

17. FERRARI 458 ITALIA

It never ceases to amaze me that car designers can create a new model that is even more stunning than the masterpiece it replaces. Such talent ... The 458 is the replacement for Ferrari's everyday supercar, the F430, and it's even more desirable. It's hard to imagine that in another decade there will be a successor that's even more covetable.

ABOVE: The view a bunny would have if it were caught in the Italia's aggressively-designed headlights.

"It's got an even more addictive sound than ever ..."

I first clapped eyes on the 458 Italia as it was undergoing some final pre-launch testing at Alfa Romeo's Bolocco test track in northern Italy. I was there with a handful of other motoring journalists to drive the new Alfa 8C Spider. Although the Ferrari was wearing some camouflage for added secrecy, its distinctive exhaust pipes were the biggest giveaway – they sit three in a row and I think they are my favourite feature.

The engine comes a close second, though, sitting in the middle of the latest rear-drive chassis. It's a V8 similar to the one in the Ferrari California, but it's bigger at 4.5-litres and has more power – 570bhp that peaks right near the top of the rev range (at 9,000rpm) and so encourages you to make it scream in each gear. You'll need the longest main straight of a Formula-One track to use all the gears like that, though – or an empty German autobahn.

Like the California, it has a super-slick seven-speed twin-clutch gearbox (there is no manual option), but its performance is swifter to 62mph, taking 3.4 seconds. At almost £170,000, it is more expensive and more powerful than the car it replaces, topping up its top speed to over 200mph. The torque has increased, too, to make the car as user-friendly as possible. It's got an even more addictive sound than ever, so being quiet while driving this car is not possible. Which surely is a good thing.

When it comes to handling, if the 430 was a peach then the 458 is peaches with added cream. A new suspension set-up and quicker steering give it an even crisper turn-in that's rarely seen this side of a racing car. As with most modern Ferraris, there's a small button called the "manettino" that controls the gearbox, traction control and suspension settings so the driver can choose which best suits the road conditions and it also lets you take control of the car's traction if you fancy sliding it round some bends. It is comfortable on the supermarket run as well though, which means you don't have to have the talents of Michael Schumacher on every trip.

Although it'll never be as practical as a family car. The running costs are more in-line with one than before, thanks to an average fuel economy of 21mpg and emissions of 307g/km CO_2. But it's the performance figures that will make the 458 Italia the most desirable Ferrari of the moment.

THE FACTS

Engine: 4.5-litre V8

Performance: 0–62 mph in 3.4 seconds, 202mph

Price: £169,546

16. FERRARI F40
15. FERRARI ENZO
14. FERRARI F50

I guarantee every car-loving boy or girl will look at any one of these three supercars and say "Wow!" I'm doing it now, even at an age when I should show more restraint, but I can't help it because these cars were made to drop jaws. You'll never forget the first time you clapped eyes on a F40 and for me, it was as a wide-eyed teenager at Goodwood Motor Racing circuit in 1990. I circled the car for a good ten minutes, salivating at this aerodynamic work of art.

"All 400 of them were sold before any rolled out of the factory..."

The F40 really is a wow car. It's a supercar with a superstar presence so dominant it could overshadow a showroom of Lamborghini Gallarados. It's one of the greatest cars ever to wear the prancing horse on its low nose. Based on one of Ferrari's other greatest, the 288 GTO, it combined road and racing talents in a celebration of the company's 40th birthday. What a gift.

In the back was a 3.0-litre twin-turbocharged V8 with 478bhp that hit 60mph in 3.9 seconds and kept on to 200mph. To keep the car's weight to a minimum and maximise the power, the interior was pretty basic but still wonderful.

As I clambered eagerly into the one at Goodwood, I clearly remember pulling the door shut using its handle – nothing more than a horizontal string of plastic. It needed the sacrifice, though, because it helped to keep the car's weight down to just over 1000kg, the same as a Fiat 500. My two-lap passenger experience was ferocious, noisy and fabulous, and as my racing driver pilot showed how fast and rewarding it could be on a track, it came as no surprise that most of its near-1,300 owners competed in theirs.

Ten years later Ferrari celebrated its fiftieth birthday with another treat, the F50, in 1995. What an even greater gift! This time it was a hard-top convertible, powered by a modified 4.7-litre V12 Formula One engine from 1992. It produced 521bhp and was as close as mere mortals could get to the performance of a F1 car on the road. Only 349 were made at the company's HQ at Maranello in Italy, and came with a price of £330,000 – about half the cost of the McLaren F1 supercar. The Ferrari's brakes and suspension were F1-derived, its non-assisted steering as precise as you'd get this side of a circuit, making the F50's talents surpass even those of the mighty F40.

Formula One technology also helped in the making of the company's 2002 Ferrari Enzo, named after its founder. It was built to celebrate the marque's first F1 World Championship of the new Millennium. Those boys know how to reward hard work. All 400 of the £418,000 car were sold before any rolled out of the factory, though demand was so high that more had to be built.

Its 6-litre V12 engine pumped 660bhp via a F1-derived semi-automatic gearbox to the rear wheels. This gave it a 0–60mph time of 3.1 seconds and a top speed of more than 220mph. The car went on to inspire the Ferrari FXX race car and be the base for the Maserati MC12.

LEFT: In full laughter mode as I get my sticky little mitts on a F40 for the second time in my life. It, together with the Enzo (above left) and F50 (above right), could just be the most perfect birthday presents ever made.

THE FACTS

Engine: 3.0-litre V8 (F40), 4.7-litre V12 (F50), 6.0-litre V12 (Enzo)

Performance: 0–60 mph in 3.9 seconds, 200mph+ (F40), 0–60 mph in 3.1 seconds, 200mph+ (F50), 0–60 mph in 3.1seconds, 220mph+ (Enzo)

Price: £163,000 (F40), £333,000 (F50), £418,000 (Enzo)

13. BENTLEY CONTINENTAL FLYING SPUR

This is such an easy car for me to include, because it was the one that whisked my brand-new husband and me away from the church after we were married. So I can tell you how cavernous and exquisitely comfortably it is in the rear, and how sumptuous the leather seats and soft floor trimmings are. Launched in 2005, it's not as large or as luxurious as the grand-daddy of chauffeur-friendly cars, the Rolls-Royce Phantom, but the four-door Flying Spur earns its moniker by satisfying the needs of both passengers *and* drivers as well.

"The interior's a bit like a boudoir too, if you're into cow hide."

U p front there's almost as much legroom as there is behind, which instantly makes you relax and look forward to the longest journey possible. I drove it for three hours solid on some of the UK's most boring motorways, but felt more refreshed as I scampered out of it at my destination than when I started. It's like sitting in your own bed within a mobile pied-à-terre.

The interior's a bit like a boudoir too, if you're into cow hide. Instruments are bold, practical and displayed in the orderly fashion that you'd expect from what is essentially a chauffeur's office. And what a desk to sit at.

I've also steered the 2,572kg (two and a half tonnes) beast across the undulating B-roads throughout Dartmouth and it behaved with the poise I'd expect from a BMW 5-series. Of course the sheer size limits its speed through very twisty lanes, but the four-wheel-drive grip makes up for its weight penalty here.

Performance figures are as impressive as its regal looks, with 60mph all yours in just under five seconds, helped by its two turbochargers and almost as much torque as horse power. It's as punchy as a 100-metre hurdler from the off. If you're game enough, it'll max out at 194mph. It's only available with Bentley's six-speed automatic gearbox, but it's one of the few fast cars that wouldn't really benefit from a manual. The six-speed automatic transmission is from the Volkswagen Audi Group anyway, which refuses to get ruffled, no matter how urgently you kick-down the throttle or pull at

the steering-mounted gearbox controls. It's such a refined system that sometimes you have to pay attention to really notice that it's actually changed gear.

The engine is a whopper – Volkswagen's 6.0-litre W12, which is shaped like a "W" by having its 12 cylinders designed in four rows of three cylinders – it also powers VW's Phaeton, which is a whole lot of car for not a lot of cash, especially second-hand, but I digress. It comes with a mouth watering 552bhp, which is more than most Ferraris.

Now that's some boast.

LEFT: Just by looking at this car you know how quiet and refined it's going to be. And it doesn't disappoint.

THE FACTS

Engine: 6.0-litre W12-cylinder

Performance: 0–60 mph in 4.5 seconds, 194mph

Price: £135,000

12. AUDI R8

Of the hundreds of car launches I've had the fortune to attend as a Road Tester for various car magazines and TV shows, my favourite has to be the Audi R8 in the South of France a couple of years ago. The biggest reason wasn't because I'd be driving the new Audi V10 engine that had just been added to the company's first-ever supercar, though that was a close call ... but because my driving enjoyment wouldn't be hampered by any film crew, demanding director, or even a stills photographer for the first time in my career. Unique bliss.

TOP RIGHT: The R8 finally gave the Porsche 911 something to worry about and extended its range with a Spyder version that went on sale in 2010 for £112,500.

"... Audi's clever team made sure its handling mimics a rear-drive chassis ..."

I didn't waste a second and took off on the three-hour test route with an audible heartbeat and an itch on my right foot that needed scratching. I found a three-mile stretch of tree-lined straight road to do just that. Heaven.

The R8 is a multi-award winning car, not the least of which was *Fifth Gear*'s Car of the Year in 2007, with its original 4.2-litre V8 engine. The latest mid-mounted 5.2-litre V10 addition to the line-up was brimming with just over 500bhp, and I felt every one of them as I reeled in the horizon and relished my solitude. It's silky-smooth power delivery and the constant feedback from every part of the car focused my mind so I thought of nothing but the R8.

From the outside you'd be forgiven for being intimidated by the aggressive look to the aluminium body. It may be just over four feet tall, but it takes up a fair width of tarmac, and those side vents that ram cool air into the mid-mounted engine help give it a presence few cars can pull off. The interior, though, is one of the most welcoming this side of your own front room and it seems to shrink around you, no matter what size.

Beneath your own well-supported rear end sit the same foundations that form the basis of Lamborghini's Gallardo and that includes Audi's quattro set-up. But because the R8 has to compete against a luminary of the car world as well as the supercar arena – Porsche's 911 – Audi's clever team made sure its handling mimics a rear-drive chassis as much as possible, so you can move its backside out of line to oversteer gracefully.

Ease off, and it relaxes into a comfortable cruiser that Bentley would be proud of – and all this from a supercar that will hit 60mph in less than four seconds and won't stop until it's almost, but not quite kissed 200mph. The V8-powered R8 is only a whisker slower, and for those of you who like to get a tan while whizzing past scenery, a convertible is available, though its lack of roof adds weight to its price, and it's the most expensive in the range at around £112,000.

With its first foray into the supercar world, Audi has drawn from its Le Mans racing know-how and from the company's extensive portfolio to give us a serious Porsche 911 rival – it's just a tiny bit softer round the edges, also making it an easy everyday car. Which should keep celebrity football owners out of the hedges as their talent diminishes away from the pitch.

THE FACTS

Engine: 4.2-litre V8,
5.2-litre V10

Performance: 0–62 mph in 4.6 seconds,
187mph (V8)
0–62 mph in 3.9 seconds,
197mph (V10)

Price: £82,555+

11. AUDI QUATTRO

The retro BBC drama *Ashes To Ashes* has given a second lease of life to its star car, the shiny red Audi Quattro that first found fame in the real 1980s. One of the most iconic motors of the decade, and not just because it looked the nuts, it has a rally pedigree that includes the World Rally Championship titles in 1982 and 1984, thanks to Audi's world-first of mating a turbocharged engine to permanent four-wheel-drive. Quite why a German company picked the Italian name for "four" – quattro – I'm not sure, but the name was given to all subsequent Audi cars with 4wd, with a lower case "q". Only the original was Quattro, and that was because someone mistakenly wrote it with a capital "Q" on the stand at the car's launch on March 3, 1980.

"… what more could Gene Hunt and his gang want? "Fire up the Quattro", indeed."

The car evolved along with the rally regulations and although it started the decade with 300bhp, it had almost doubled by the end of it. Michele Mouton became the first woman to win a world rally in an Audi Quattro, but it wasn't just because of her that I paid a keen interest in the car. I was a massive motorsport fan as a kid and my parents drive an Audi 80 – the car on which the Quattro was based, albeit with Audi 200 suspension and brakes. So I spend many hours looking at the four-rings on the grille and pretending my mum was Michele Mouton and Dad was the 1984 World Rally Champion, Stig Blomqvist. The imagination of an 8-year-old, hey.

The road-going version of the Quattro had a five-cylinder engine with just under 200bhp. It was capable of hitting 60mph in 7.1 seconds and a top speed of 137mph. I know the majority of family saloon cars boast these facts and figures nowadays, but back then the roads were full of Austin Metros, so the Audi really was something special.

I had the treat of driving one along twisty Welsh lanes for *Fifth Gear* and it lived up to my hopes of being fabulous and fun. There's loads of grip when you set off, as you'd expect with the Quattro system ensuring the power to all four tyres, helping each corner dig into the tarmac. You'd need to find some proper dusty tracks to get it skipping and hopping à la Blomqvist, though.

LEFT/ABOVE: A strong contender for the world's worst piece of parking. The Quattro is definitely a contender for one of the world's most iconic cars.

It wasn't the most sophisticated car of its time to drive though – gliding into the lead in that respect was Jaguar's XJS – and I certainly noticed a lack of smoothness in almost every area. The gear changes were not-so-seamless, the power delivery slightly rough, but I didn't care too much as I buzzed from the thrill of driving one of my idols. It's quite practical as well, with two sculpted rear seats and a reasonable boot, so what more could Gene Hunt and his gang want? "Fire up the Quattro", indeed.

THE FACTS

Engine: 2.144-litre five-cylinder

Performance: 0–62 mph in 7.1 seconds, 137mph

Price: £14,500

10. A1 GP RACE CAR

9. PORSCHE CARR

8. LOTUS ELIS

7. LOTUS

6. L

RA GT

EXIGE

AMBORGHINI MURCIELAGO

5. FERRARI 430

4. FORMULA ONE

3. BUGATTI VEYRON

2. PORSCHE 911 S

1. LAMBORGHINI DIABLO GT

10. A1 GP RACE CAR

When I was a 6-year-old, I was in the back of my father's Scimitar GTE – a bronze-coloured two-door, four-seater sports estate – as we sped along a dual carriageway nudging the national speed limit. It was the first time I really remember thinking about speed and I asked my Dad if he could show me what 100mph felt like.

"I was getting close to the maximum speed that this car was capable of ..."

He said if I *really* wanted to feel every movement, vibration, sensation and noise involved in taking a car to 100mph, the best motor would be an old Mini. Fifteen years later I did just that. As ever, Dad was right – it left me with a re-arranged skeleton.

Since then my speed-quest threshold has doubled to 200mph, and I've been trying to reach it for the last 10 years, making films for *Top Gear* and *Fifth Gear*. My first attempt was in an Aston Martin Vanquish S (see pages 120–121) and my last crack at it was in a single-seater racing car from the A1 GP championship. The A1 GP was described as the "World Cup of Motorsport" because each car represented a country, but sadly it has now folded due to the economic climate.

However, in 2007 I borrowed the brightly-coloured A1 GP car from Team Ireland – they went on to win the title in the final year – and the smooth runway of RAF Cottesmore in Rutland. The Lola B05/52 was powered by a 3.4-litre V8, built by motorsport engine gurus Zytec, and in the right conditions it was capable of 200mph.

It was only a few months after Richard Hammond's horrific crash, which happened as he was trying to break a straight-line speed limit. And although he had been strapped to a much more powerful machine, his misfortune lingered in the air.

As I strapped into the racing harness, in full racing overalls and helmet, the V8 throbbed into life. The cameras recorded my trip to the start-line and others lurked along the runway ready to capture my run. It was a tense, thrilling moment as I drew up to my start position and I was sitting so low to the ground that I couldn't see the end of the runway through the heat haze. I unleashed the car in a blast of noise and hoped to hit the fastest speed I had ever experienced in my life.

As soon as the revs maxed out in first gear, I threw it into second, then third and fourth. The engine was screaming before each change, the steering and seat vibrating like crazy. I snatched a millisecond glance down at the digital Speedo to make sure it was still rising quickly enough and I was wringing everything I could out of it. Fifth gear came and went in a blur, so I seized sixth and the final gear, and that was all that stood between me and the big 200. I felt a push from the side due to the crosswinds on the open airfield as the Speedo read 180mph. I still had a good third of the runway ahead, so it was looking good.

182, 185, 187mph as the revs neared the limit. I was getting close to the maximum speed that this car was capable of here today, and just hoped it would be enough. 188, 189, 190mph – I was so close I could lick it. And then ... nothing. Zilch. The revs were at their absolute limit and I could physically go no faster.

From my experience of racing karts as a teenager, I knew different gear ratios gave either good top speeds for fast circuits, or good pull-out-of-corners on tight and twisty ones, so I suggested we fit a different sixth gear. Unfortunately, though, we didn't have one on site and our filming logistics meant we didn't have the time to source one. So my current record stands at 190.1mph. Which I'm still quite chuffed about.

LEFT: I was really touched when I saw the Team Ireland boys had troubled themselves to put my initials on, but sadly I couldn't quite touch the magic 200mph.

THE FACTS

Engine: 3.4 litre V8

Performance: 190.1mph

Price: Not for sale

9. PORSCHE CARRERA GT

For me, this car is right up there with the super-giants like Ferrari's F40 and Lamborghini's Diablo GT. It's an absolute diamond among the greatest cars in the world because of two main reasons – it's fantastically driver-focused and is, perhaps, the best-engineered supercar of all time.

ABOVE/RIGHT: The entire production run of this superb peice of engineering was sold out before a single car was built.

Almost 1,300 were made, and every one of them sold before it was even built and – a rare fact for a car like this – the Carrera GT actually made the company some money. Launched in 2003, its engine was a 5.7-litre V10, originally destined to power a Porsche Le Mans racer (a project which failed to be realized in 2000), so it's a seriously potent piece of kit. So much so that the clutch is made from ceramic to best cope with the 612bhp and 435lb ft of torque.

It's a tricky car to get smoothly off the line without either stalling it or roaring off in a cloud of smoke, which I'm sure would be most peoples' preferred exit. It has a 0–62mph time of 3.9 seconds and a top speed over 200mph, which puts it in the mix with most supercars and not too far behind the Ferrari Enzo and McLaren F1. Accompanying the Carrera GT's figures are the most wonderful screams and shouts from the V10; they are so intrusive they'd make a Monk blaspheme.

Floor the throttle and make sure you're hanging on because you'll catapult forward with enough force to send you into warp drive. It's ferocious, phenomenally fantastic and seemingly never-ending. Across country, it's an involving, demanding and ultimately testing car for your skills as well as nerve, and the more you focus on driving it, the more it'll pay you back with its superb handling, solid body control and great grip. It's a wonderfully balanced car.

Another key to its gut-punching performance is its trim weight. The passenger cell is made from carbon fibre and the targa-type roof removed in two panels that are almost finger-tip

light. Seats are feather-like too, and the rest of the cabin is just as well thought through, with enough leather and aluminium to make you feel special but not over-the-top.

Which is how you could describe the exterior, too. The car is not as eye-catching or as detailed as a Pagani Zonda, nor does it have a rear end as flamboyant as the F40's, but the Carrera GT has been designed to be as functional as possible. It is perhaps the best-finished supercar of all time, combined with outstanding engineering that makes it less of a supercar and more like the world's first hypercar.

THE FACTS

Engine: 5.7-litre V10

Performance: 0–62mph in 3.9 seconds, 205mph

Price: £320,000

8. LOTUS ELISE
7. LOTUS EXIGE

When the little Lotus Elise was first launched in 1995, I went to the company's headquarters at Hethel in Norfolk to speak to designer Julian Thompson and vehicle architect Richard Rackham. They loved riding high-performance motorbikes and were impressed at how the lightweight frames and powerful engines gave them an urgent sense of speed and freedom that you couldn't get from just any car.

"I think it's fantastic"

So they designed one that could, and now I always think of the Elise as a sort of four-wheel bike. Aluminium construction formed part of its design. Some of this was left exposed in the cabin, with no carpets to cover the welds either. This went some way to keeping the car's weight to a minimum, just like a bike.

Its 725kg was originally combined with a 1.8-litre Rover K-series engine, also a popular choice for its two-seater Caterham rival. Even though it had just 118bhp, chicken feed for a sports car, this was enough to make the Elise the ultimate pocket rocket. It changed the rules for how we expect a sports car to handle and has remained at the front of that field for 15 years. During its time it has evolved, of course, but it still looks as sharp and clean now as it did at the launch and I think its design is as ageless as the ultimate icon of the skies, Concorde.

I first tested an Elise for *Top Gear* and couldn't believe that something that went so quickly and handled so perfectly was road-legal and wasn't a racing car. I was astonished that here was a car that seemed to be an extension of my body and mind, and almost anticipated my desires before I did. Because the car is so small and well-packaged, there's zero delay in your orders being carried out. Turn the wheel and the tyres turned; push the throttle and the speed increased instantly. Even the suspension was on top of ironing out road bumps before you knew you'd hit them. I was seriously impressed with this petite machine from Lotus.

I drove it all day on the picturesque country roads of Gloucestershire, but I saw very little of the scenery as I was sitting so low down, busy concentrating on the next bend, and the next and the next. It was so good that Vauxhall demanded a copy of it. The VX220 was commissioned and became the halo car for the entire Griffin-badged range. Lotus also thought the Elise good enough to base two further cars on, the slightly more practical Europa coupé and the track-focused Exige, which is also a coupé but for those who drink petrol for breakfast.

It looks fantastic, with its roof air scoop and rear wing, and carries no flab around its flanks. It's equally as pert to drive, with no sign of any body roll or any slack in the steering, brakes or throttle. The 2.0-litre Toyota engine is supercharged and it loves to rev in each of its six gears. It's the perfect car for track days and would be the ideal motor in which to embarrass a few Ferraris in the right hands, as its 0–62mph figure of 4.0 seconds makes it ripe for a F430 race.

It's not the most practical car, though, as you'll have to grease yourself up before climbing in or out of it, and the rear visibility is close to zero. It does come with a cup holder, but if you drive it properly, you won't have time for a slurp. I think it's fantastic.

LEFT: The brunette beside me in the Elise is my older sister, Lottie, whom I tried to teach to drive quickly around a racing circuit for *Fifth Gear*. I tried.

THE FACTS

Engine: 2.3-litre four-cylinder

Performance: 0–60 mph in 3.1 seconds, 155mph

Price: £42,900 (CSR260)

6. LAMBORGHINI MURCIELAGO

The Lamborghini Murcielago will always hold a special place in my life because it's the car in which I taught my mum Valerie how to drive round a racing circuit. She was brilliant. Another film for *Fifth Gear*, it came about because we wanted to highlight the fact that Lamborghinis had become really easy to drive since Audi took over, just around the new millennium.

ABOVE: From this angle it reminds me of the killer shark, Jaws – its sharp snout and predatory manner are scary but equally thrilling. **RIGHT:** The V12 is picture perfect in the back.

"With a little encouragement we were off and Mum was driving a Lamborghini!"

The Murcielago (pronounced *mercy-ell-ago*) was the replacement for the Diablo and die-hard Lambo enthusiasts, including my fellow TV mate Tiff Needell and I, were worried that Audi would suck out their Italian souls. But the Murcielago still looked like something that had just landed from Uranus, which was a very good omen. More importantly, Audi had injected a much-needed shot of German build quality.

Its finely honed bodywork retained Lamborghini's signature scissor doors that guarantee a spectacular arrival. Of course, the sound of its 6.2-litre V12 engine announces your approach a long time before. At £158,000, it was launched with Lamborghini's first six-speed manual gearbox, which was four too many because it could quite easily hit 90mph in second gear. It took four seconds to reach 60mph, and if you did use all the cogs it would blast onward to 205mph, which is not bad for a company that started out making tractors.

It was not all such good news for the hard-core fans because it was fitted with four-wheel-drive and traction control – two aids that strike fear into any decent pilot. But it did have the capacity to send 90 per cent of its 507bhp to the rear wheels, which softened the blow somewhat. Then, a few years later, there was a new addition that featured a bit of electronic wizardry called "e-gear", a semi-automatic gearbox so easy to use that, apparently, anyone could drive it. And so cue my mummy, who drives nothing but the old farm Range Rover with its auto box stuck firmly in the "drive" position.

First of all, I showed Mum how easy it was to slide the car on a wet Welsh Anglesey race track (just in case she'd ever wondered how it was done, which I doubt very much). Much as I was loving, loving, loving the combination of the car's great chassis and even greater engine, my passenger wasn't. If looks could kill ... So before her stomach became detached, we swapped seats. With a little encouragement we were off and Mum was driving a Lamborghini! She'd married a former British kart racer and produced two racing drivers children in her time, yet she's barely reached the national speed limit, let alone crossed it.

I set her the challenge to go round the circuit in one-and-a-half minutes. After a few laps at the pace of a sleeping tortoise, Mum's confidence grew and she found the paddle-shift gear changes incredibly easy. We even reached third at one stage ... She embraced the experience with guts and after more encouragement, managed a lap in one minute and 25 seconds. And so together that day, the original VBH and I proved that the Murcielago has the talent to suit all talents.

THE FACTS

Engine: 6.2-litre V12

Performance: 0–60mph in 3.4 seconds, 211mph

Price: £222,126 (latest)

5. FERRARI 430

In 2004, Ferrari's mainstream 360 motor was replaced by the F430, available in both hard- and soft-top Spider form. It's powered by a 4.3-litre V8 with 483bhp and almost as easy to use everyday as a Fiat Punto, thanks to top-drawer technology, steering-mounted gear shifts and delightful steering. But with Ferrari's background in motorsport, one of the strongest in the world, it wasn't long before a racing version was made.

"… just 49 seconds to race round one lap with an average speed of 85mph …"

Called the F430 Challenge, Ferrari made enough of them to compete in a one-make championship against each other, and in 2009 I achieved a lifetime's ambition of racing one. Now when it comes to a racing car, or road car for that matter, my wish list is short, but sweet – a good engine and a good chassis. Good night. And that's what the F430 is blessed with.

The steering is one of the most accurate and perfectly-weighted of any car I've driven. The rear-wheel-drive chassis is so well-balanced and so capable of putting that power onto the track, through its 19-inch slick racing tyres, that it has become one of my favourite cars ever. In addition to such surefooted handling, the racer was fitted with an aerodynamic-boosting rear spoiler of dinner-table proportions and a carbon-fibre front splitter that would give Bruce Forsyth's chin a run for its money.

The engine remained untouched, but the car's weight was reduced by 200kg to help boost its agility out of the corners and to make it 2–3 seconds-a-lap quicker than the street-legal car. Lightweight plastic replaced most of the heavier glass and carbon fibre went in place of as much of the cast iron as possible. F1-derived parts were used too, including "contractive" dampers that contain a spring that acts like an anti-roll bar to eliminate body roll and pitch. You can't see them, but you can certainly feel how well they keep the body tight to the tarmac in even the tightest turns.

I was racing at Brands Hatch circuit, in a Championship open to all supercars, not just F430s. The circuit twists its way over 1.2 miles in length, but it took just 49 seconds to race round one lap with an average speed of 85mph – a very quick dash to the shops.

The field of 26 cars was divided into four different classes depending on engine size, and I was in a class of eight, battling for honours against other F430s and lots of Porsche 911 GT3s. During qualifying, I was the fastest Ferrari out there, and so started the 25-minute race near the front of my class but sixth overall on the grid. And in the race, after a big battle with a 911 GT3, who hit my passenger door with such force it sent me into a massive slide, I romped home to finish second in class (fourth overall) and put my hands on a trophy in my Ferrari race debut. What a dream come true!

LEFT: Racing the Ferrari was one of the best experiences of my competitive career, topped off with taking home some silverware.

THE FACTS

Engine: 4.3-litre V8

Performance: 0–60 mph in 4.0 seconds, 196mph

Price: From £139,000

4. FORMULA ONE

Not many people get the chance to even touch a Formula One car, let alone drive one, but my F1 portfolio includes two drives and a pair of passenger rides in specially-designed multi-seater versions. Ever since I was racing karts as a 12-year-old I dreamt of being a Formula One driver. F1 represents the best of everything in the car-racing world and it's where the teams and drivers push their engineers, designers, mechanics and fitness trainers to find the slightest, slimmest, smallest advantage that will gain the tinniest fraction of a second per lap. It's where a lot of road car technology is developed along the way, too.

ABOVE: They don't look like this any more: I drive a Formula One car on a 1.3-mile race track. **RIGHT**: Interviewing 7x World F1 Champion Michael Schumacher, for *Fifth Gear*.

"After just three laps my neck muscles ached for the following two days."

The two Formula One cars I was so, so lucky to drive weren't state-of-the-art machines because they would have been too precious for mortals like me to tank about in, so I was let loose in cars that had raced about eight years previously and definitely weren't near the front of the grid when they did. But I didn't care because they were still Formula One machines with back-snapping acceleration and soul-splitting sounds.

The first F1 experience was in an AGS car filming for *Top Gear* in the late 1990s at a circuit in France, which cleverly didn't have a main straight long enough to test the car's top speed. The second time was for a feature in the *Daily Telegraph*, where I was in an even-older Formula One car and at the even-smaller circuit of Mallory Park in Leicestershire. Both times I'd been with a small group of people who needed nothing more than a fair bit of cash to drive some of fastest racing cars on earth.

Strapped tightly in, the acceleration was more physical and more brutal than I'd ever experienced and the tyres seemed to stick out like planets on my eyeline, but I saw them respond instantly to the smallest of my instructions. The super-firm chassis means you feel each tiny bump in the road and your senses are so alert and awake to every movement that it's like having an out-of-body experience. The people running these experiences are smart enough not to give you enough laps for you to become too confident in the machine, but it was just long enough to scare and thrill me in equal measures.

The best time I had, though, was in the back of a purpose-built Arrows F1 two-seater with Mark Webber at the helm. It was at Donington Park race circuit and after just a few seconds of hard acceleration, the air in my chest had been punched out, my helmet pinned back and I was scared stiff but absolutely loving it.

And when we came to the first sharp corner, where I thought Mark must have passed out because he missed my usual braking spot by a week, when he finally decided to brake my head flew forward and my neck muscles strained to pull it upright again, such is the phenomenal G-forces the car creates as it slows dramatically from 200mph. After just three laps my neck muscles ached for the following two days.

Today's race cars are fitted with 2.4-litre V8s, which rev to 18,000rpm (a normal road car peaks at about 7,500rpm) with around 800bhp, that are thirsty enough to see the fuel economy reduced to 4mpg in a race. Another amazing fact about the most incredible car in the world.

THE FACTS

Engine: 2.4-litre V8

Performance: 0–60mph in a nanosecond, 200mph+

Price: £priceless

3. BUGATTI VEYRON

For a car to be named "Car of the Decade" by BBC's *Top Gear*, it has to be good. The Bugatti Veyron is, and then some. It is a car that makes grown men wobble at the knees and it makes my pulse quicken just at the sound of its name. It's the car that every schoolboy and girl wants in a game of Top Trumps because it's pretty much unbeatable. It's exactly the kind of machine you dream of as a kid as well, and the only way you could perhaps make it even better is if it sprouted a pair of wings and flew too. But as it is, a car you can commute to work in and pull a jet-ski with at the weekend is a pretty wonderful invention.

"It's like being strapped to a rocket, where tunnel vision becomes the norm."

Built between 2005 and 2008 in coupé form, this mid-engined, four-wheel-drive supercar has made it into my top three because of its staggering facts and figures. Here goes: it's powered by an 8.0-litre W16 with not one, but four turbochargers, 64 valves, four camshafts and three exhausts. If that wasn't enough to get you all feverish, it also has almost 1,000bhp. That's more powerful than a Formula One car by a healthy 200bhp – and you can drive the Bugatti to the shops.

It's got almost as much torque, too, which helps it to say hello and goodbye to 62mph in 2.5 seconds. It won't stop punching a hole in the atmosphere until it reaches 253mph – making it, at the time, the fastest street-legal production car. It needs a mere 5.5 seconds to hit 100mph, and 16.7 seconds to nudge 186mph from a standstill. I can barely make it to the sofa in that time. It's like being strapped to a rocket, where tunnel vision becomes the norm.

Its stylish looks are made up of perfect curves to minimize drag on its way to those superstar speeds, and it's packed with some clever technology as well. As the speed increases, the car's ground clearance drops via hydraulics from 12.5cm to 6.5cm nearer the tarmac. Giving it traction are specially developed Michelin tyres that are hideously expensive to replace or repair – you can buy a Porsche 911 S for the cost of replacing a set.

When it comes to slowing down, the Veyron has the equivalent stopping power of a performance car on each of its four corners, thanks to carbon ceramic discs. There's the added safety of having the anti-lock braking system fitted into the handbrake, should some manual intervention be required. The rear wing also snaps into action to scrub speed, much like the wings on an aeroplane when it lands, so it can slow so rapidly – 2 Gs of deceleration – that you'll be hanging out of the seatbelt.

With Bugatti owned by the VW group, the Veyron has the company's dual-clutch DSG (Direct Shift) gearbox with shift paddles behind the steering wheel. It's so sophisticated that it takes just 150 milliseconds to go from one gear to the next all the way through its seven gears. Fuel consumption is 7mpg at worst, and almost 12mpg at best. If you prefer a more visual idea, it would empty its 100-litre fuel tank in just 12 minutes at full throttle. What I'd give to find a road that would sustain a 250mph blast for that long.

One final top trump stat for this magnificent beast is its price – a cool £840,000. But around 200 people throughout the world haven't been put off by that, and although the Coupé isn't on sale any more, it has been replaced by the Grand Sport and its removable top. When I win the Lottery...

LEFT: The car's so fast it has slipped through my fingers and remains on the top of my most wanted list of cars to drive.

THE FACTS

Date: 2006

Engine: 8.0-litre W16

Torque: 978bhp

Performance: 0–62 mph in 2.5 seconds, top speed: 253mph

Price: £840,000

2. PORSCHE 911 CARRERA S

As a motoring journalist, I am oh-so-fortunate to be given cars to test by manufacturers. However, Porsche, quite wisely, stipulate journos must be at least 25 years old before they can drive one, which meant I had to wait a long time for my first professional test. It was worth it, though.

"It's the purist's dream that requires a degree of talent to drive it hard and fast."

I was at the launch of the latest variant of the 911 at the time, the Targa, with its sliding glass roof that combines the elements of a cabriolet with a hard-top coupé. I'd always been a fan of 911s, something I inherited from my father, and from the moment I sat in that Targa, my appreciation and love of the German model was reinforced. Big time. The range is pretty extensive now and includes four-wheel-drive, turbocharged, race-ready and soft-top version. The one I love best is the simple 911 S model, priced at a comparatively lowly £72,000.

Being rear-wheel-drive, it's a purist's dream which requires a degree of talent to drive it hard and fast, as opposed to models with four-wheel-drive safety nets. It's powered by Porsche's unique-sounding six-cylinder 380bhp engine that will slingshot the car to 60mph in 4.7 seconds, and on up to 188mph.

It is one of the most intuitive cars I've ever driven. The steering knows where you want it to be almost before you know yourself, and the feedback from the tyres is so complete that you almost get a print of the road on your palms. The steering has perfect weight to it as well, which makes you wish all journeys had eternally sweeping right-left-right bends.

The handling is electrifying and invigorating. I've tested one at Silverstone racing circuit and had the rear end sliding from one corner to the next, thanks to a well-timed stab of the throttle and a never-ending juggling act with the wheel. Porsche 911s used to have a reputation for being snap-happy at the back end, but they have become less unruly over the generations. They still set your senses on fire, though.

The six-speed manual gearbox (the automatic is brilliant, but I love being in full control) works as an extension to your wrist, which is pretty much the ethos for the rest of the car – it

becomes your motorized appendage. But no matter which one you go for, the 911 is a car that has been designed for maximum driver pleasure in the cabin too, from the wraparound seats to the rev counter smack-bang in the middle of your eyeline.

It's remarkably comfortable on long journeys and there's even room for a full-size adult in the back – albeit for a limited amount of time. I know this because I folded my mother-in-law into the rear for one and a half hours before the complaints started. And, randomly, of the thousands of cars I've washed in my duties as a Road Tester, it's the one car I will never tire of cleaning. Its bulges and curves are a chamois leather's delight!

LEFT: The 911 Carrera S came within a whisker of the top slot in my sexy 100, but it is a fantastic bit of kit. If only my hips were as well-sculptured.

THE FACTS

Engine: 3.6-litre six-cylinder to 3.8-litre turbo

Torque: 493bhp (turbo model)

Performance: 0–60mph from 3.7 seconds (Turbo), up to 193mph (GT3)

Price: £64,300–£104,000

1. LAMBORGHINI DIABLO GT

As the last millennium drew its final breath, the fastest and most expensive ever Lamborghini had just been born – the Diablo GT. No other production car in the world could beat its 211mph top speed, as the 230mph McLaren F1 was no longer being made. More than a decade later, it remains my answer to a frequently-asked question: "What's your favourite car?"

ABOVE: My #1 – and looks set to remain as such for eternity. **ACROSS, BELOW**: The very one I drove for *Top Gear.* If you look closely you can see me in the driver's seat.

While working as a presenter on BBC2's *Top Gear* programme, I flew to Lamborghini's HQ at Sant' Agata in Italy for my date with destiny. The Devil (*Diablo* is Italian for devil – how apt!) was parked outside one of the main buildings opposite Lambo's must-visit museum. I had just spent an hour dribbling in there, and as I walked out to see the car for the first time, goose bumps shot over me.

It's a seriously intimidating sight: all £195,000 of it. It's not terribly tall, but that only adds to its vast length and width – 4.5 metres by 2.2 metres – and it's covered in angular panels, scoops, vents, spoilers and side skirts.

Someone with a sense of humour had painted this one yellow. Hardly mellow.

As with all super-duper supercars, the door pivots forward and skyward, adding to its already-dramatic shape. That was the moment when my nerves overshadowed my excitement. Never again has a car had that effect on me – and I've gone on to test Formula One cars.

The BBC TV crew fitted the car with on-board mini-cameras and sound-recording gear to capture all my precious moments behind the wheel. As carefully as you put a sleeping baby to bed, I slipped down into the shapely sports seat of the left-hand drive car and remembered to breathe. I gazed in awe at the width of the dash and was shocked at how far away the passenger door was from where I sat. The transmission tunnel was a prominent feature, splitting the cabin down the middle, and the pedals felt as though there was a galaxy between each of them.

With enough pent-up excitement to blow a hole in the GT's low roof, I fired up its 6.0-litre V12 engine and revelled in its growl, childishly "blipping" the throttle to scare myself again and again. With 575bhp it takes just a whisker over three and a half seconds to reach 60mph. It needs just three seconds to go from 30mph to 70mph in third gear. These are lung-punching times – and the raw roar from the V12 scatters the air around you, becoming all you can hear. Or want to.

The five-speed gearbox needs a bit of Girl Power to move through and the steering wheel requires a strong grip to keep from veering off over grooves and bumps in the road when you're pushing on. Sneeze at speed on a country road and you'll be sorry! The turn-in is crisp and the 18-inch tyres grip really well … but as soon as we found a disused airfield to film at, the GT and I danced in figures-of-eight and doughnut rings, smoking rubber with ease.

It's a car that's very hard to drive slowly – the power and noise are too addictive. The suspension isn't soft enough for mundane motorway trips, either. This is a car that needs the open road. Fewer than 100 Diablo GTs were ever made and the car has an intoxicating hold on me that no other has yet managed to shake.

"… as I walked out to see the car for the first time, goose bumps shot over me."

THE FACTS

Date: 1999

Engine: 6.0-litre V12

Torque: 569bhp

Performance: 0–60mph in 3.7 seconds, 202.6mph

Price: £195,000

LAMBORGHINI
GALLARDO LP 570-4 SUPERLEGGERA

This bright-green Lamborghini cover car is a sight for sore eyes in so many ways. Its "Kermit The Frog" colour won't be the most popular choice among too many buyers (if any), but I think it just highlights the fact that this Gallardo is special.

Called the LP 570-4 Superleggera, it sits at the top of the model range and sports a "superlight" badge that tells the world it's as light as possible to be as fast and as agile too. Lamborghini think of it as a "lean automotive athlete" and it's set to be just as popular as its predecessor, which was launched in 2007 and sold 618 cars in just over a year.

This latest Superleggera is 70kg lighter than the already-trim Gallardo LP 560-4, which makes it the lightest road-going car the Italian manufacturer currently makes at 1,340kg, fact-lovers.

Helping to keep the fat off are lashings of carbonfibre, inside and out – the spoiler, sills, diffuser and mirror casing are all made from this super-strong material, and then there's the aluminium body, which saves weight too.

The majority of the glass has been replaced by a special plastic, including the engine cover which frames the V10 power unit like the

RIGHT: I can't think of any other manufacturer that could get away with such a lairy paint job, and it suits this Superleggera brilliantly.

THE FACTS

Engine: 5.2-litre V10

Performance: 0–62mph in 3.4 seconds, 202mph

Price: £180,000

work of art it is. However, creature comforts are still on offer in the form of electric windows and air conditioning – two weighty features I'd happily sacrifice to extract that last drop of performance.

LP in the car's name actually stands for "longitudinale posteriore" and refers to the position of the 5.2-litre engine – it's mounted longitudinally (as opposed to transversely) behind the driver. It packs a fabulous 562bhp, which helps it get from zero to 62mph in 3.4 seconds. It will then go on to hit 124mph (200kph) in 10.2 seconds and won't stop until it's seen 202mph.

The six-speed automatic e-gear transmission has steering wheel paddles and they slide through the gears faster than any human could do, with a traditional manual shift – but that's a no-cost option, if you want it, and I think I would, just because I like to have full control.

If you feel the need to show off at the traffic lights there's a Thrust Mode, where the car will sit at 5,000rpm and once the lights go green, roar off with minimal wheel-spin into the distance.

The LP 570-4 Superleggera also comes with Lambo's four-wheel-drive system, which offers an enormous amount of cornering grip, especially in the wet, but still manages to keep the hardcore rear-drive fans interested by having a 30:70 front-to-rear power split in normal conditions.

It's a serious piece of kit, with a serious price tag of £180,000. And having spent a day with this particular one shooting for my book cover, I've fallen for the colour and think it's priceless.

FERRARI
599 HGTE

Ferrari's 599 is one of the most accomplished and admired grand touring motors ever to wheel out of Italy. The engineers' brief was to make a car that exceeded the performance of the F40 – a tough ask.

But this near-£225,000 machine not only achieves that, thanks to its 611bhp 6.0-litre V12 engine derived from the Ferrari Enzo, but it's also one of the most refined and spacious Ferraris ever: two words you don't normally associate with products from the Prancing Horse. Its handling is superb as well, which makes it one of the most desirable cars ever.

But if you think it's not desirable enough, then how about this more expensive, more driver-focused version called the 599 HGTE (Handling GT Evoluzione)? You pay an extra £14,000 (plus *whatever* takes your fancy on the never-ending options list a £383 fire extinguisher or £827 suitcase might tempt you) but there are more tell-tale differences that let others know you've bought the best.

For starters, the HGTE sits on 20-inch split-rim alloy wheels, there's a choice of five colours for the brake callipers that sparkle within, and there's the two-tone tail-pipe and matt-black diffuser.

Step inside and there are carbonfibre seats with specially designed leather and Alcantara trim – "HGTE" embroidered, of

RIGHT: No matter which model the Prancing Horse adorns, Ferrari manages to capture the spirit of motoring in every one and not least here with the 599.

THE FACTS

Engine: 6.0-litre V12

Performance: 0–62mph in 3.7 seconds, 205mph+

Price: £221,884

course, more carbonfibre around the dash and a white background to the rev counter.

Then there's the multitude of improvements that aren't so visible. The ride height is 10mm lower, the suspension is stiffer and tyres give more grip. The Formula One-derived gearbox has even quicker changes, taking just 85 milliseconds to move from one gear to another (the standard 599 needs 100 milliseconds).

Performance figures are pretty impressive, too, with a 0–62mph time of 3.7 seconds and a top speed of more than 205mph – that's certainly more impressive than the F40, but not quite as quick or as fast when flat out as the Enzo.

Around Ferrari's own test track at Fiorano in Italy, the 599 HGTE is just over half a second quicker than the 599 and that's also thanks to new software that improves the car's accelerator response, as well as giving it an even boomier exhaust note.

It's an intoxicating car to be in from the moment the engine fires up and these modifications make a great car even greater. The pursuit of more speed and such hard-core handling does create a small casualty, though in the form of the car's ride, which is not as comfortable as other GTs, but I reckon that's a compromise well worth paying.

MORGAN

ROVER MG F

TWIN-EN

T

INED LVW GOLF

UCK RACER

GIBBS AQUADA BOAT CAR

CITROEN 2CV 24-HOUR RACER

MORGAN – ALL OF THEM

Car manufacturers have definitely raised their game in the last decade and now even the smallest and cheapest car on the market isn't too awful to drive. The safety levels have increased enormously as well as the level of standard equipment on offer, too.

I have driven my fair share of shockers over the years, including an Asia Rocsta, which was a small, four-wheel-drive, off-road-type of vehicle from Korea, but its ride was so harsh and unbearably uncomfortable that I was surprised to get out of it with my skeleton still intact after just a few miles. It's not made anymore.

There have been plenty of others with very poor handling and second-rate fixtures and fittings, but without doubt the worst I've had the misfortune to spend time in was a Morgan.

These British-built, hand-crafted motor cars boast a history that's over 100 years old and they have one of the biggest and most loyal followings of any manufacturer. Also, there's a waiting list of a couple of years before you can even take delivery of a new one.

However, I won't be joining it because of what happened when I took one for a spin in the late 1990s – the steering wheel actually fell off as I was driving it and that's inexcusable for any vehicle, let alone a sportscar.

It was a Morgan Plus 4 and I was driving it close to the company's HQ in Malvern, Worcestershire. I'd spent a pleasant enough day meandering through the peaceful country lanes, doing my best to connect with the car's Olde English image and pace. But then it came toward the end of the day and the steering wheel fell forward from the steering column and was left hanging on by a thread. I can laugh about it now but it tainted my thoughts on the car, though to be honest I wasn't too impressed with it before that happened.

It was built in Morgan's traditional way of putting an Ash frame over a steel chassis with aluminium coachwork and running boards along both sides. It looks like something more at home in a Miss Marple mystery than modern Britain – and it still looks, and is built the same way today.

But its handling isn't as reassuring and as chuckable as you'd expect from more traditional sportscars and the ride is bordering

"… the worst I've had the misfortune to spend time in …"

on the super-firm. And then there's the refinement, or lack of it, because the noise of the 2.0-litre engine, gearbox and wind are intrusive. And when it comes to comfort, this barely reaches an acceptable level as it's rather cramped in the cabin and because, ironically, of the steering wheel that won't adjust (unless I'm driving it) and feels too close to you.

Such is the passion of Morgan owners that I know I will be upsetting a lot of people here. Ooops!

LEFT/ABOVE: A Morgan with its steering wheel in the correct place, and despite the image of adventure, I got more than I bargained for when I took one for a spin.

THE FACTS

Engine: 2.0-litre four-cylinder

Performance: 0–60mph 7.5 seconds, 120mph

Price: £31,706 (latest)

ROVER MGF

When Rover launched its two-seater sportscar in the mid-1990s I was working for *Auto Express* magazine as a Road Tester. I remember being quite excited about driving the company's spiritual successor to the incredibly successful MGB, which had been sold throughout the 1960s and 1970s.

ABOVE: I'm not sure if the sight of a MGF or a Morgan makes me want to barf more. And Rover had the audacity to thrust its machine upon the racing world.

"… the ladies gave it a resounding thumbs up, loving its design, quick and simple roof operation …"

It was Rover's big hope to reinvent and capitalize on the much thought-of octagonal badge which, thanks to the fondness most people had for the MGB, epitomized British sportscars. And in a clever move to do its best to recapture that admiration instantly, the MGF shared a similar design to the 60s icon.

It was an affordable soft-top that hoped to appeal to anyone with a keen interest in the heritage of the brand and also to women – so much so that the magazine invited my mother and a handful of other women along to drive a MGF to gauge their opinions.

After driving it around the Chobham test track in Surrey for half a day, the ladies gave it a resounding thumbs-up, loving the design, quick and simple roof operation and the fact that the MG badge gave the car a credible, upmarket image.

I could not have disagreed more strongly. To me, the Rover MGF was a car that was trading on the long–gone exhaust smoke of the MGB and it wasn't as good as Mazda's current MX-5. The interior of these early MGFs was poorly thought-through and attention to detail was not a high point; the driving position was awkward as well, with a high seat and non-adjustable steering wheel that made sure tall drivers weren't welcome.

To be fair the engines – ranging from a 1.8-litre 120bhp to a 1.8-litre 160bhp – revved well and were reasonably responsive and probably this car's best feature. The five-speed manual gearboxes were notchy and when you have the super-slick action of the MX-5's gear change to compare with, it makes you wonder what the chaps at Rover had actually used for inspiration.

And then there was the handling which, thanks to the car sitting on a hydragas suspension system that was fitted to Rover's Metro, made it roll too much for a sportscar and failed to make it as lively and as agile as its Mazda rival.

And even when Rover launched the MGF racing series, which attracted a lot of up-and-coming young drivers, it still didn't manage to lift the car out of my least favourite pile, where it has remained to this day.

In the early 2000s it evolved into the MG TF and that model is still produced today, but it won't be making an appearance in my dream garage.

THE FACTS

Engine: 1.8-litre four-cylinder

Performance: 0–60mph 8.4 seconds, 127mph

Price: From £13,799 to £16,399 (latest MG TF)

TWIN-ENGINED VW GOLF

There are very few cars I've driven that make my heart physically sink when I look back at the time I spent in them. But this Volkswagen Golf does just that, even full a decade after I took it for a spin.

"... it shot off with the ferocity you'd expect from such a powerful car – it can reach 60mph in 3.2 seconds."

It was in 2000 when I was that year's featured guest in Jeremy Clarkson's DVD, *At Full Throttle*. We were filming some great-handling cars at an airfield in Gloucestershire, including a Nissan Skyline and Subaru Impreza. And then there was this Golf.

At first glance, the light-but-bright-blue car looked exactly the same as you'd find in a VW showroom, but open the door and the similarities ended right there. There were no soft carpets, door pockets or even roof linings. All the comfortable seats had been ripped out and only two of them had been replaced – by high-backed racing ones complete with a racing harness.

In the back instead was a 2.8-litre VR6 engine from VW, but it had been turbocharged to give 325bhp. There was no cover over the engine so I could actually see it move about in its "engine bay" when we were on the move.

Now I know there's nothing too radical about having an engine in the back of a car – it's what Porsche has done with its 911 for years – but with the Golf, what made it unique was an identical unit in the front of the car too. So, all in all, this little machine had a whopping great power total of 650bhp – more than a Lamborghini Gallardo.

There were two gearboxes as well, which Dub Sport, the company responsible for this monster, tried hard to merge into one gearstick in the traditional position between the seats, but it didn't have the smoothest operating action.

Firing up the pair of engines was a very noisy affair and I had to shout to be heard on the DVD over the constant chatter and bark coming from both ends of the car.

I pointed the Golf in a straight line, hit the throttle and it shot off with the ferocity you'd expect from such a powerful car – it can reach 60mph in 3.2 seconds. Toward the end of the runway, I started to slow the speed and I was then hit by the smell of oil and the sight of smoke from the engine sitting right behind me, where the back seat should be, turning the experience into one of the smelliest, hottest and most unpleasant trips of my life.

And then I tried to turn the car around, still carrying some speed, and realized that this particular VW was built for going in straight lines only, restricting its habitat to a drag strip. I was very glad to get out of it.

LEFT/ABOVE: These pics are taken from the DVD which is why they aren't super-sharp. But even if they were, they'd still look blurred because the Golf is a bone-shaker.

THE FACTS

Engine: 2.8-litre VR6 turbocharged – two of them

Performance: 0–60mph in 3.2 seconds

Price: Too much, whatever the cost

TRUCK RACER

One very sunny morning a few years ago I drove to Brands Hatch racing circuit in Kent to drive the largest, most powerful and biggest-engined vehicle I've ever driven – a full-on racing lorry. I was really keen to drive it but also a whisker apprehensive because I've never looked at a heavy good vehicle on the motorway and thought 'ooh, I simply must drive one of them as they look so agile'. Powerful yes, but nifty round the bends? Definitely not.

ABOVE: Definitely the tallest vehicle I've had the pleasure of taking round a track and it out-handled many cars I've tested.
ABOVE RIGHT: Regular racer Stuart Oliver leading the charge in a race.

So order to make them more agile and less of a Health & Safety nightmare, there are no long trailers attached though the sight of them swinging uncontrollably about during a race would certainly be an entertaining one! But truck racing is fabulously impressive to watch as it is.

My machine for the day was a MAN TGA, which was powered by an unbelievably huge 12-litre turbo diesel engine that gave out a staggering 1,050bhp. That's so much more than a Formula One car's 800bhp, but even more incredible is its torque at 5,000 Nm (Newton metres). A Lamborghini Murcielago has 660Nm (487lb ft) and that's one of the most potent machines on our roads.

The truck was owned and raced by the nine-times British Truck Racing Champion Stuart Oliver – an instantly-likeable man, who clearly has a lot of truck talent. He showed me round the 5,300kg beast first and explained how the engine alone was worth close to £100,000.

The gearbox was the biggest I'd ever seen, with 16 gears, but that doesn't equate to a high top speed because these trucks are limited to 100mph for safety racing regulations. But that does mean you can go round a corner at 100mph. The whole thing weighs 6 tonnes and therefore needs special water-cooled brakes to keep them from buckling during a fiercely-fought race.

That weight, though, is kept as low to the ground as possible to help keep it stuck to the track and as resistant to toppling over as possible. And it does this brilliantly.

After I'd grabbed and stood on anything I could get hold of to haul myself up and into the cabin, Stuart showed me the ropes for the first couple of laps and I was instantly impressed with the truck's stability and agility round the 1.2-mile twisty track. But what really shocked me was the g-forces, the likes of which I hadn't experienced since my two-seater passenger Formula One ride with Mark Webber, a few years previously. Incredible.

Stuart set a lap time of almost 62 seconds, which was to be my goal, and so in a race helmet, suit and strapped in tightly, off I

went. You don't use all 16 gears once you're up and running, just the relevant few, but the key to a fast lap was keeping the revs between a lowly 1,500rpm and 2,000rpm because that's where all that juicy torque was at its peak. The rev limit comes in a 3,000rpm anyway – way short of a normal turbo diesel car's of around 5,500rpm.

I had to remember to put my foot down a few seconds before I actually needed the power because that's how long the turbo lag took to come and go. I couldn't get over how fantastic it was to handle, though – just like a great sportscar – and when the back end of the rear-drive truck did slide out on the exit of a 90 degree left-hand bend, it was so progressive and incredibly easy to bring back into shape. Looked great, too!

My lap time came down to 65 seconds, then 64 seconds and after a lot of concentration I managed a shade over 63 seconds – not as quick as Stuart, of course, but good enough to have put me fourth on the starting grid at the previous year's Brands Hatch truck race. I loved it.

THE FACTS

Engine: 12-litre six-cylinder

Performance: 0–60mph in 7.0 seconds, 100mph

Price: £100,000 engine alone

GIBBS AQUADA BOAT CAR

In the early 2000s I had my first and only taste of a car that turns into a boat, just as you'd expect to see in a James Bond movie... It had the aquatic name of Aquada and was built by a British-based company called Gibbs and was designed to have the handling of an 'average sportscar' on the road and a leisure boat on the water.

ABOVE: This is the solution to that troublesome question I know we all ask - 'darling, should we buy a car or a boat?'.

It was, and remains, my most unusual road test, not least because of the unusual way I had to get into it – there are no doors so I hopped over the fixed sides and into the cockpit. Then there's the seat layout, which is like that of a McLaren F1 road car, with the driver's one in the middle and slightly forward of the two passenger seats. This design may be fancy-looking but it's actually incredibly practical because when the car becomes a boat, it's the perfect fit to take out a driver, a waterskier and an observer.

It's powered by a 2.5-litre V6 engine which is enough to see it to 60mph in under 10 seconds on the road – not as fast as I'd expect from a similarly-powered sports car, but the Gibbs Aquada sits high off the tarmac and weighs more than a normal car and both these factors slow it down. It has a four-speed automatic transmission, sits on 16-inch alloys and runs on normal unleaded fuel.

There's definitely a big element of fun when you drive it because it looks so unusual and therefore gets a lot of attention. It drives reasonably well, but the Gibbs' marketing boys were right when they said it was like an "average sportscar". It's not going to win any agility tests on tarmac, but there's nothing off-putting about it at all.

Eventually the road part of my test ended by driving down a slipway and at the edge of a lake. By the water's edge I pressed a button and drove slowly onward, keeping the revs at about 2000rpm to provide enough thrust to the jet as we went in. On the water, the engine's powers disengage drive from the rear wheels to drive a compact 40kg jet to propel it through the water. This expels one ton of thrust, which is enough to see the Aquada reach almost 35mph.

Within seconds the car's wheels had moved to a horizontal position (exactly as you'd expect in a Bond movie) and we were off. It was surreal and brilliant, especially as I was being splashed by ice-cold water when just moments ago I'd been rushing past green hedgerows.

In this guise the Aquada's trim tabs and bilge pumps were called into action from their on-road redundancy. The pumps remove water that's taken on and the trims are plates attached to the rear of the "boat" that push down on the water to help the thing skim over the water.

I felt it was fast and seriously good fun, and so did a certain Richard Branson because in 2004 he used a Gibbs Aquada to set a new record for crossing the English Channel in an amphibious vehicle. I wish it had been me.

THE FACTS

Engine: 2.5-litre V6

Performance: 0–60mph sub-10 seconds, 100mph

Price: £150,000

CITROEN 2CV 24-HOUR RACER

In the early 1990s I took part in one of the earliest 24-hour races for one of the unlikeliest racing cars the world has ever seen, the Citroen 2CV. The event was held at the Mondello Park circuit not too far from Dublin in Ireland and it's one of the friendliest-run tracks I've ever raced at – highlighted by the fact there is a pub at the end of the pit lane which sells Guiness, of course.

" … I certainly noticed a lack of smoothness in almost every area."

The only long-distance race I'd done beforehand was 24 hours in a lawn-mower powered kart – which I reckon was quicker than the Citroen. I was part of a four-man driver team some of whom had raced the year before, and the plan was to drive as fast as we could and swap over at various fuel fill-ups throughout the day and night. Simple.

The car was without a doubt the slowest I've ever raced with its slightly tweaked 2-cylinder 602cc engine squeezing 35bhp out of it and mated to a 4-speed manual gearbox. The front-wheel-drive car had the skinniest 15-inch tyres I've ever raced on too, and the understeer was chronic.

The cars are narrow, which encourages them to go round a corner three or four abreast which is fantastic fun to be amongst, but perhaps even better to watch from the safety of the grandstand. Or bar stool. Tucking up close the bumper in front of you meant you could get a great 'tow' into the vacuum of air in front and then slingshot out to overtake at the end of the main straight, and this action was seen right throughout the racing pack of around 40 cars. 2CV racing is certainly entertaining.

The cars are lighter and sit about five inches lower than their road-going siblings and their suspensions are certainly stiffer. But their body roll is still so exaggerated that it's comical, and even more so when you're driving it round really tight bends and hanging on to the steering wheel in the hope you won't roll over. Plenty did though during my race but the cars are made of such thin metal that the marshals simply pushed them back onto

LEFT: There's not a lot of difference between the go-anywhere road car and the track-oriented racer. Just some stickers really.

their wheels to join the racing once more. Pre-race we qualified somewhere towards the last third of the field and drove as fast we possibly could – flat-out in these 2Cvs can top 95mph with the wind behind you. Whatever speed though they sound like children blowing raspberries.

After my first incident-free stint at twilight I managed a few hours' sleep in trackside tent and remember being woken all too soon for my next session. Off I went once more and after almost 900 laps our team took the chequered flag, finishing in the top 20.

It was definitely the most leisurely-paced races I've ever competed in, and one of the most fun.

THE FACTS

Engine: 602cc, two-cylinder

Performance: 0–60mph in 12.0 seconds, 95mph

Price: £2,000 for a race-winning car, £200 from the scrapyard

INDEX

A

A1 GP Race Car 166–7
Abarth
    Trofeo Abarth 500 GB Racer 36–7
Ace Café 15
Alfa Romeo
    8C 102–3, 155
    8C Super 102–3
    RZ 42–3
    SZ 42–3
Andretti, Mario 107
Ariel
    Atom 80–1
Arrows
    F1 177
Aston Martin
    DB7 24–5
    DBS 124–5
    DBS Volante 109
    One–77 118–19
    V8 Vantage 124–5
    Vanquish S 120–1, 167
At Full Throttle (DVD) 199
Audi
    Quattro 162–3
    R8 160–1
    TT Roadster 26–7
Auto Express (magazine) 196

B

Bentley
    Continental Flying Spur 158–9
    Continental GT Speed 104–5
BMW 17
    507 51
    F1 Car 116–17
    M1 90–1
    M3 144–5
    M3 Cabrio 144–5

X5 68–9
Z1 50–1
Z3 M Coupé 70–1
Z4 43, 70–1
Z8 50–1
Bugatti
    EB 110 110–11
    Veyron 178–9
Butler-Henderson, Charlie 37, 113
Butler-Henderson, Guy 8, 41, 67, 87,
    166–7
Button, Jenson 139

C

Carweek (magazine) 89
Caterham
    Seven 112–13
Chapman, Colin 101
Chrysler
    Viper 20–1
Citroen
    2CV 204–5
Clarkson, Jeremy 59, 87, 109, 199
Coulthard, David 8

D

Daily Telegraph 177
Dennis, Ron 139
Dodge
    Charger 22–3

F

Fenn, David 141
Ferrari
    308 GTS 46–7
    430 174–5
    456 88–9
    458 Italia 154–5

Dino 47
Enzo 156–7, 169
F40 156–7
F50 156–7
Fiat
    500 36–7, 157
    Grande Punto SS 37
Fifth Gear 8, 15, 38, 39, 47, 51, 61, 65,
    69, 81, 85, 89, 95, 105, 113,
    117, 121, 129, 137, 143, 149,
    161, 163, 167
Filippis, Maria Teresa de 123
Fittipaldi, Emmerson 107
Ford
    Capri 38–9
    Escort RS Cosworth 142–3
    Fiesta 49
    Gran Torino 22–3
    GT 86–7
    GT40 86–7
    Mustang 18–19, 38
    Puma 48–9
    Racing Puma 48–9
Formula One cars 176–7

G

Gibbs
    Aquada Boat Car 202–3
Giugiaro, Giugiaro 91
Goodwood Festival of Speed 30, 31

H

Hamilton, Lewis 139
Hill, Damon 107
Holden
    HSV 56–7
Honda
    FCX Clarity 16–17
    NSX 140–1

J

Jaguar
   XJ220 58–9
   XJS 13
   XK8 12–13
   XKR 12–13

L

Lamborghini
   Diablo 111
   Diablo GT 182–3
   Gallardo 152–3, 161
   Gallardo 170–4
   Superleggera 186–7, 190–1
   Murielago 152, 172–3
Lancia
   Delta Integrale HF Turbo 148–9
Land Rover
   Defender 41–2
   Discovery 15
   Range Rover 40–1
Lauda, Niki 91
Lexus
   LF–A 92–3
Lotus
   Elise 31, 101, 170–1
   Europa coupé 171
   Evora 100–1
   Exige 170–1
   Exise S 113

M

McLaren
   F1 59, 150–1, 157, 169
   MP4–12C 138–9
Marsh, Matthew 123
Maserati
   Gran Cabrio 60–1
   MC12 157
   Quattroporte 34–5
   Trofeo 122–3
Masters, Robin 47
Max Power (magazine) 111
Mazda

MX–5 84–5, 197
Mercedes–Benz
   C63 AMG 94–5
   SL65 AMG Black 82–3
   SLR McLaren 55, 77, 138–9
   SLS AMG 54–5
Mitsubishi
   Evo 136–7
Morgan 194–5
Mouton, Michele 163
Murray, Gordon 141, 151

N

Needell, Tiff 38, 81, 117
Nissan
   350Z 134–5
   370Z 134–5
   Skyline GT–R 72–3
Noble
   M400 76–7

O

Oliver, Stuart 201
O'Sullivan, Ronnie 95

P

Pagani
   Zonda 130–1, 169
Pagani, Horacio 130, 131
Peugeot
   205 GTI 66–7
Piquet, Nelson 91
Plato, Jason 75
Porsche
   911 Carrera S 180–1
   911 Targa 181
   Boxster 33, 107, 128–9
   Carrera GT 168–9
   Cayenne 98–9
   Cayman 98–9, 101
   Panamera Turbo 126–7
Proton 101

R

Radical
   SR3 80–1
Renault
   Alpine A610 Turbo 52–3
   Clio 64–5
   Megane 17
   Megane Renaultsport 172 65
   Megane Renaultsport 200 65
   Megane Renaultsport 250 64–5
   Megane Renaultsport 250 Cup 65
Rolls–Royce
   Phantom 32–3
Rover
   MGB 196, 197
   MGF 196–7

S

Stevens, Peter 151
Sunday Times 13

T

Tata 13
Tesla 30–1
Top Gear 8, 26, 43, 57, 59, 73, 113, 167, 171, 183
Toyoda, Akio 93
truck racing 200–1
TVR 74–5

U

Ultimate Bad Boy (UBB) 19

V

Volkwagen
   Golf GTI 66–7
   Twin–Engined VW Golf 198–9

W

Webber, Mark 177, 201
Wheeler, Peter 75

PICTURE CREDITS

To see more of some of the cars in my book please visit my website www.butler-henderson.com and click on the section 100 SEXY CARS BOOK. You can hear them too!